Magical History Tour
Hidden Oil

FABRICE ERRE
Writer

SYLVAIN SAVOIA
Artist

PAPERCUTZ

Magical History Tour

#3 "Hidden Oil"

By Fabrice Erre and Sylvain Savoia

Original series editors: Frédéric Niffle and Lewis Trondheim
Translation: Joseph Laredo
Lettering: Cromatik Ltd

Jeff Whitman – Managing Editor
Ingrid Rios – Editorial Intern
Jim Salicrup
Editor-in-Chief

ISBN 978-1-5458-0690-6

Originally published in French as *"Le Fil de l'Histoire, Tome 4 – L'Or Noir"*

www.papercutz.com

Papercutz books may be purchased for business or promotional use. For information on bulk purchases please contact Macmillan Corporate and Premium Sales Department at (800) 221-7945 x5442.

Printed in Malaysia
May 2021

Distributed by Macmillan
First Printing

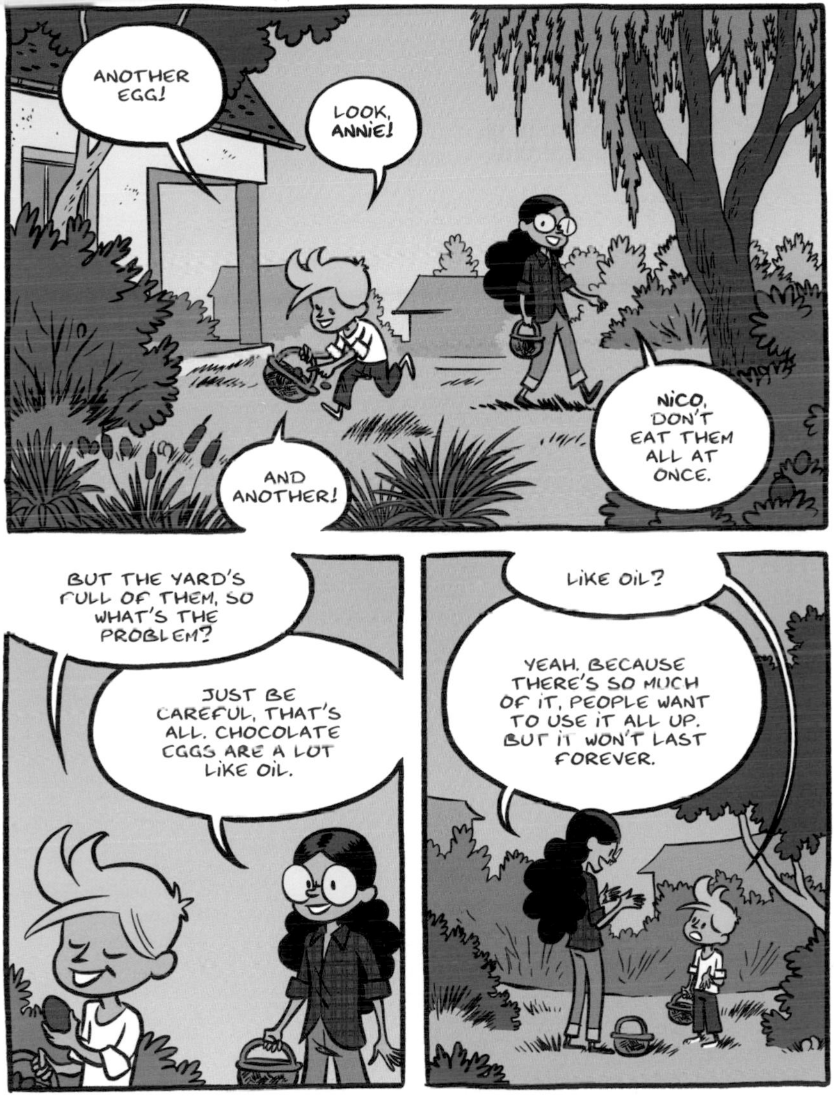
ANOTHER EGG!
LOOK, ANNIE!
AND ANOTHER!
NICO, DON'T EAT THEM ALL AT ONCE.
BUT THE YARD'S FULL OF THEM, SO WHAT'S THE PROBLEM?
JUST BE CAREFUL, THAT'S ALL. CHOCOLATE EGGS ARE A LOT LIKE OIL.
LIKE OIL?
YEAH. BECAUSE THERE'S SO MUCH OF IT, PEOPLE WANT TO USE IT ALL UP. BUT IT WON'T LAST FOREVER.

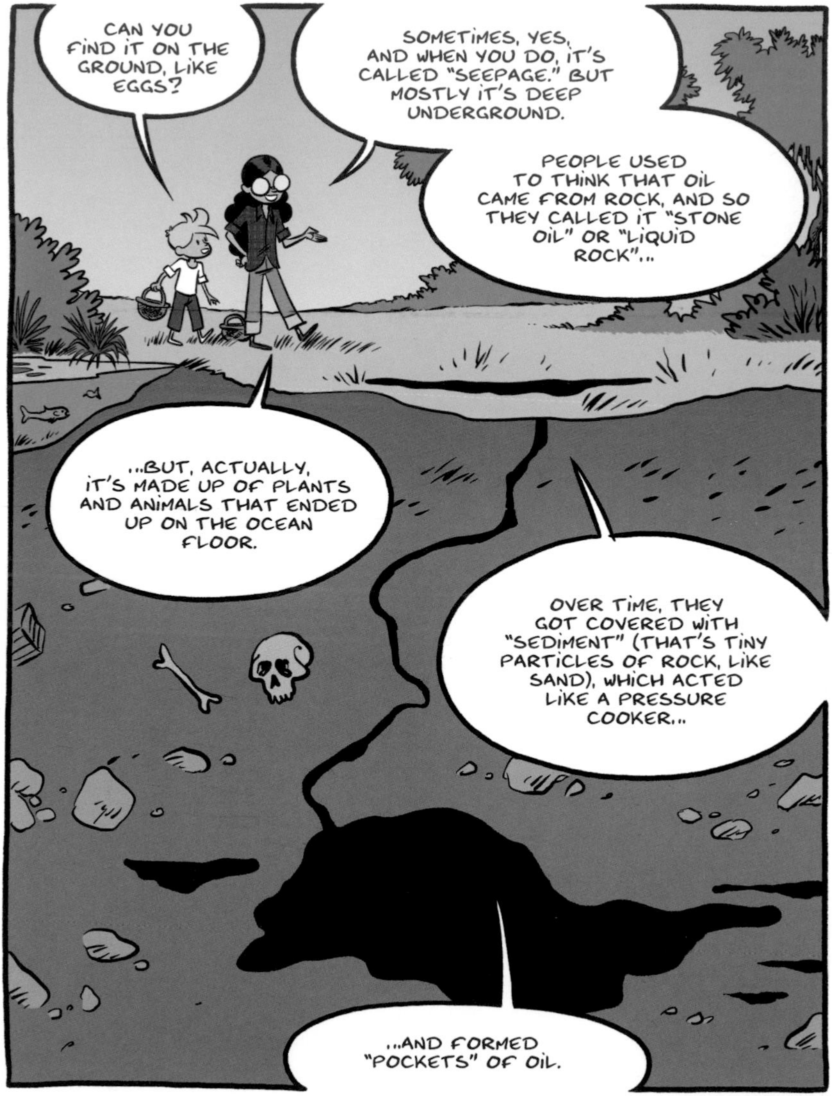
CAN YOU FIND IT ON THE GROUND, LIKE EGGS?
SOMETIMES, YES, AND WHEN YOU DO, IT'S CALLED "SEEPAGE." BUT MOSTLY IT'S DEEP UNDERGROUND.
PEOPLE USED TO THINK THAT OIL CAME FROM ROCK, AND SO THEY CALLED IT "STONE OIL" OR "LIQUID ROCK"...
...BUT, ACTUALLY, IT'S MADE UP OF PLANTS AND ANIMALS THAT ENDED UP ON THE OCEAN FLOOR.
OVER TIME, THEY GOT COVERED WITH "SEDIMENT" (THAT'S TINY PARTICLES OF ROCK, LIKE SAND), WHICH ACTED LIKE A PRESSURE COOKER...
...AND FORMED "POCKETS" OF OIL.

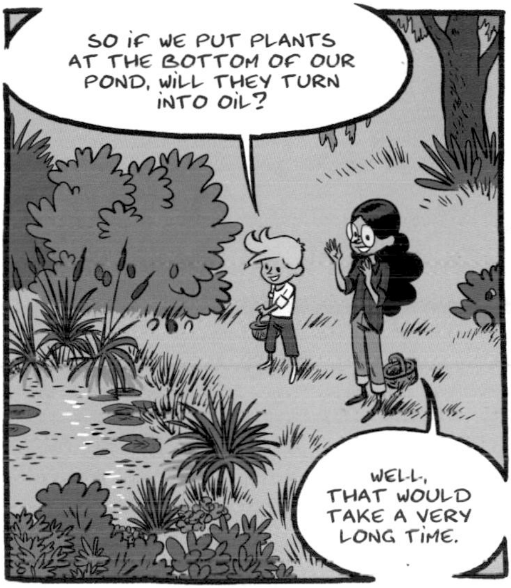
SO IF WE PUT PLANTS AT THE BOTTOM OF OUR POND, WILL THEY TURN INTO OIL?
WELL, THAT WOULD TAKE A VERY LONG TIME.

THE PROCESS OF TURNING PLANTS INTO OIL TAKES MILLIONS OF YEARS. IT STARTED LONG BEFORE HUMAN BEINGS EXISTED.

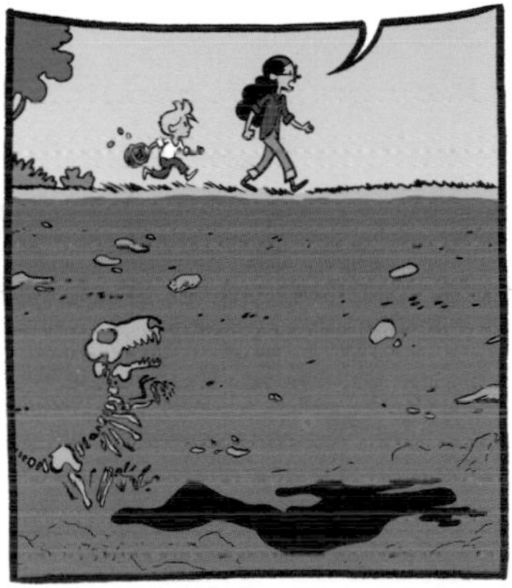

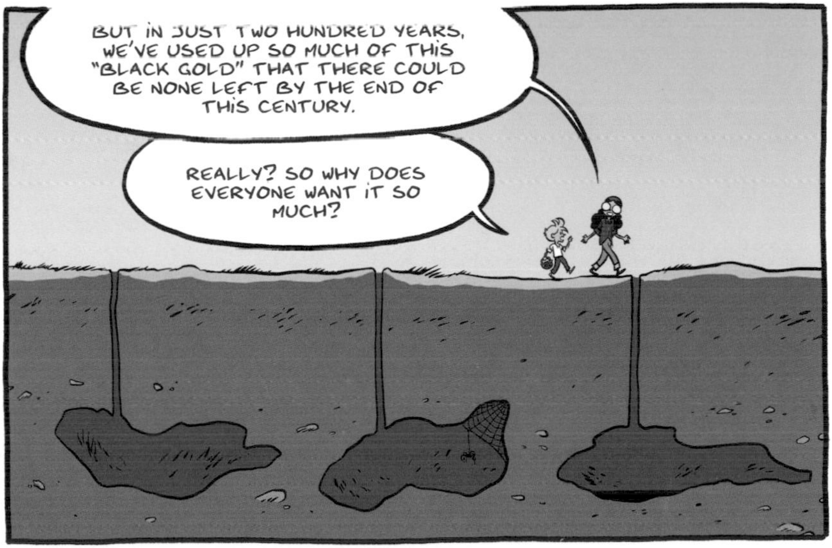
BUT IN JUST TWO HUNDRED YEARS, WE'VE USED UP SO MUCH OF THIS "BLACK GOLD" THAT THERE COULD BE NONE LEFT BY THE END OF THIS CENTURY.
REALLY? SO WHY DOES EVERYONE WANT IT SO MUCH?

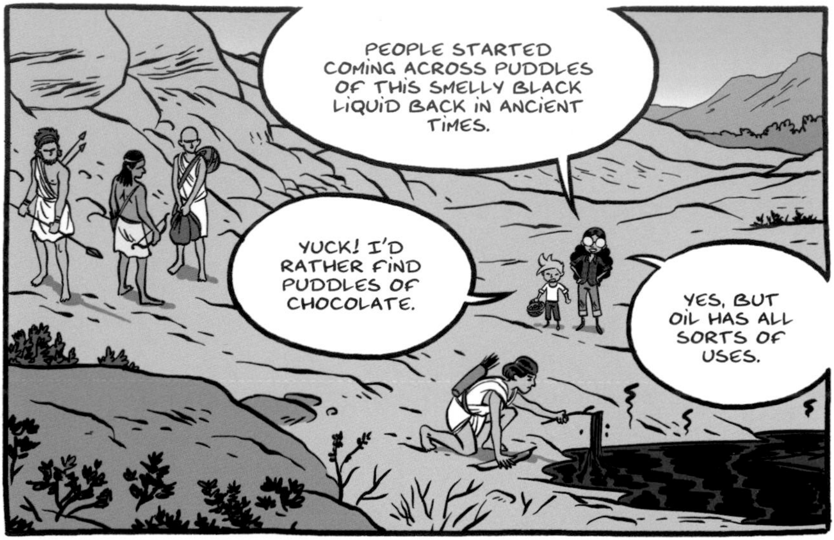
PEOPLE STARTED COMING ACROSS PUDDLES OF THIS SMELLY BLACK LIQUID BACK IN ANCIENT TIMES.
YUCK! I'D RATHER FIND PUDDLES OF CHOCOLATE.
YES, BUT OIL HAS ALL SORTS OF USES.

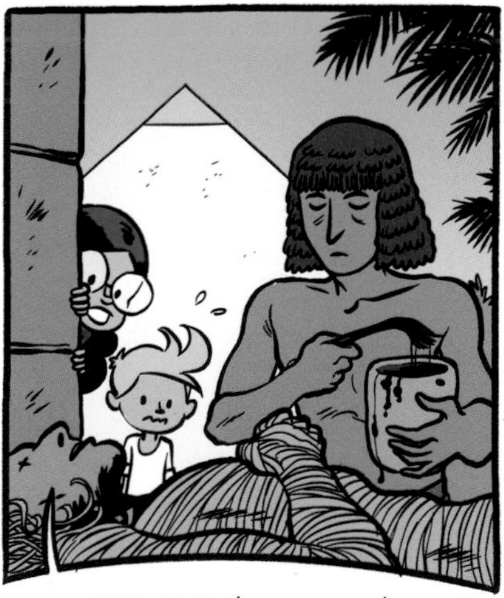

THE EGYPTIANS USED IT TO PRESERVE THEIR MUMMIES.

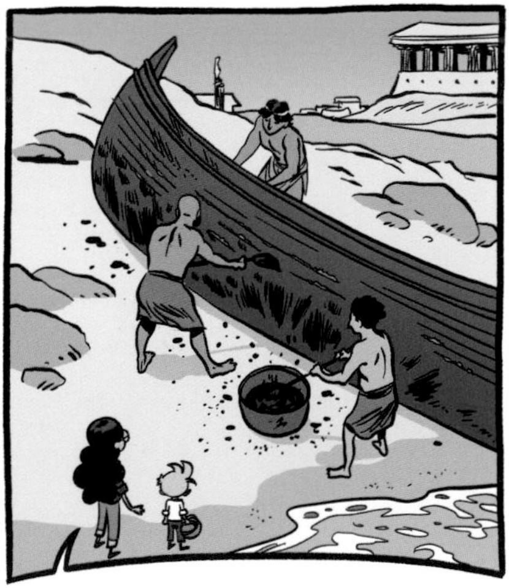

THE GREEKS SEALED THEIR BOATS WITH IT.

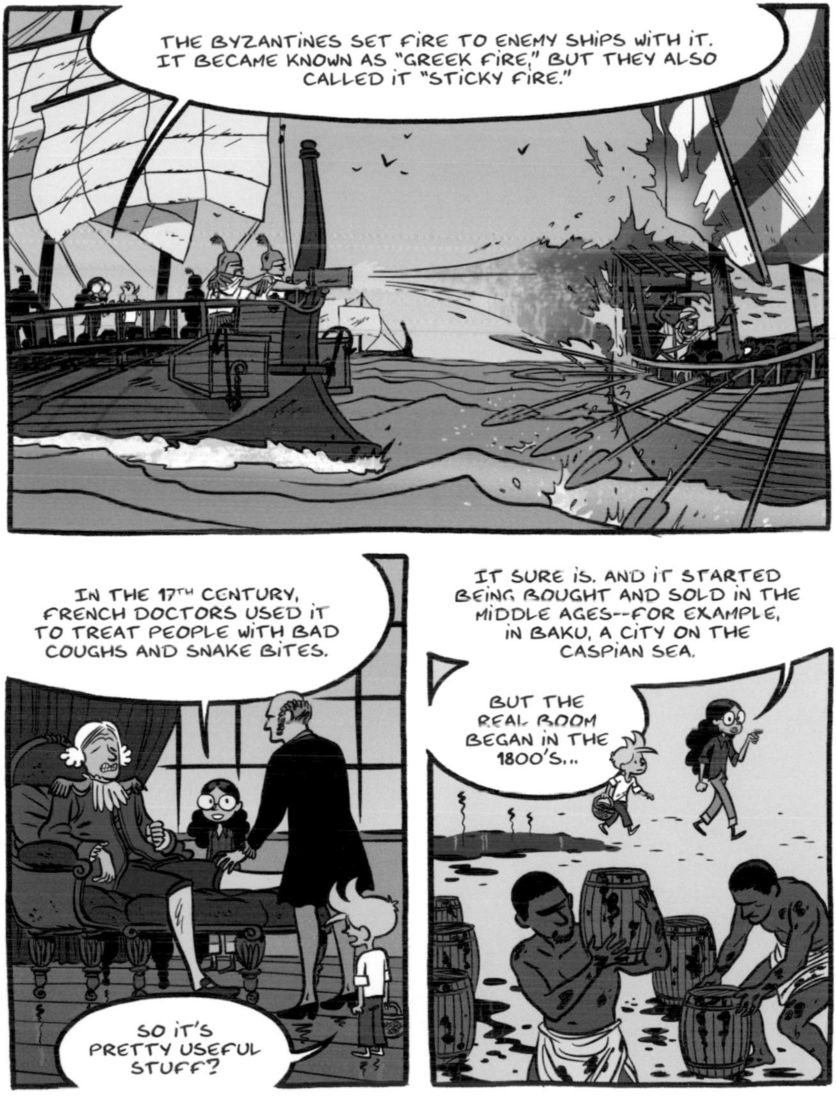
THE BYZANTINES SET FIRE TO ENEMY SHIPS WITH IT. IT BECAME KNOWN AS "GREEK FIRE," BUT THEY ALSO CALLED IT "STICKY FIRE."
IN THE 17TH CENTURY, FRENCH DOCTORS USED IT TO TREAT PEOPLE WITH BAD COUGHS AND SNAKE BITES.
SO IT'S PRETTY USEFUL STUFF?
IT SURE IS. AND IT STARTED BEING BOUGHT AND SOLD IN THE MIDDLE AGES--FOR EXAMPLE, IN BAKU, A CITY ON THE CASPIAN SEA.
BUT THE REAL BOOM BEGAN IN THE 1800'S...

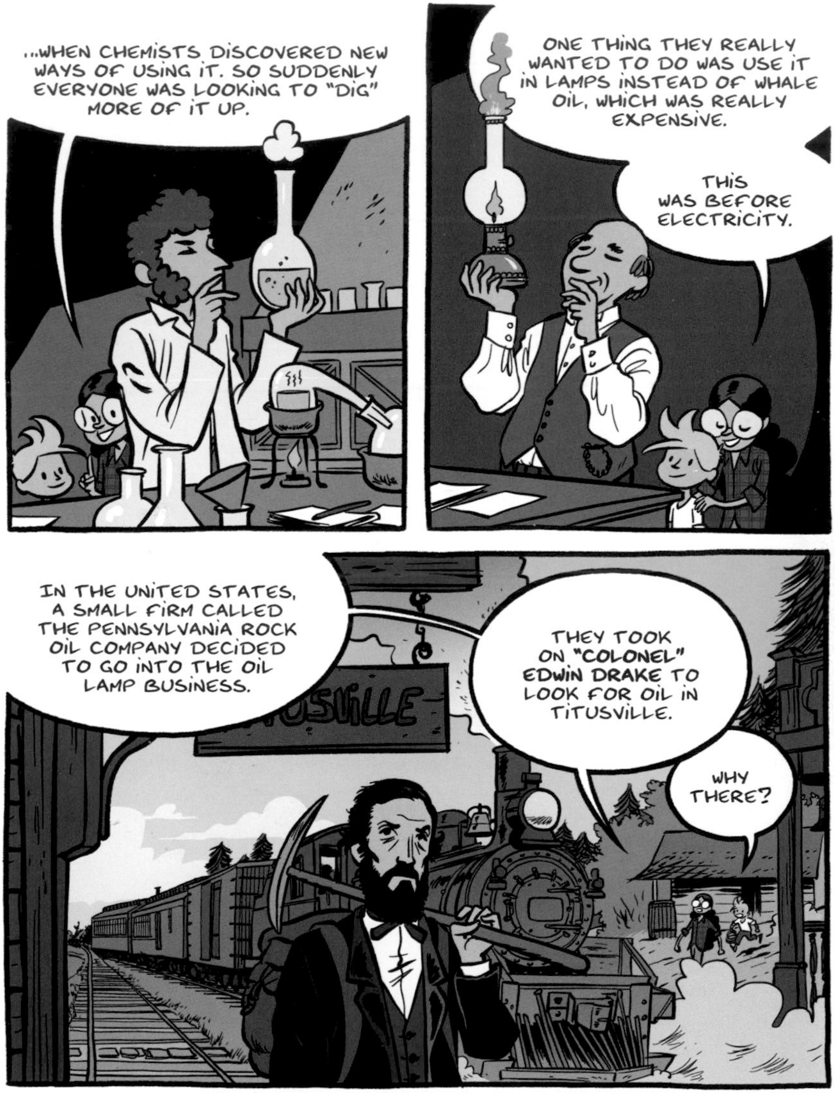
...WHEN CHEMISTS DISCOVERED NEW WAYS OF USING IT. SO SUDDENLY EVERYONE WAS LOOKING TO "DIG" MORE OF IT UP.
ONE THING THEY REALLY WANTED TO DO WAS USE IT IN LAMPS INSTEAD OF WHALE OIL, WHICH WAS REALLY EXPENSIVE.
THIS WAS BEFORE ELECTRICITY.
IN THE UNITED STATES, A SMALL FIRM CALLED THE PENNSYLVANIA ROCK OIL COMPANY DECIDED TO GO INTO THE OIL LAMP BUSINESS.
THEY TOOK ON **"COLONEL" EDWIN DRAKE** TO LOOK FOR OIL IN TITUSVILLE.
WHY THERE?

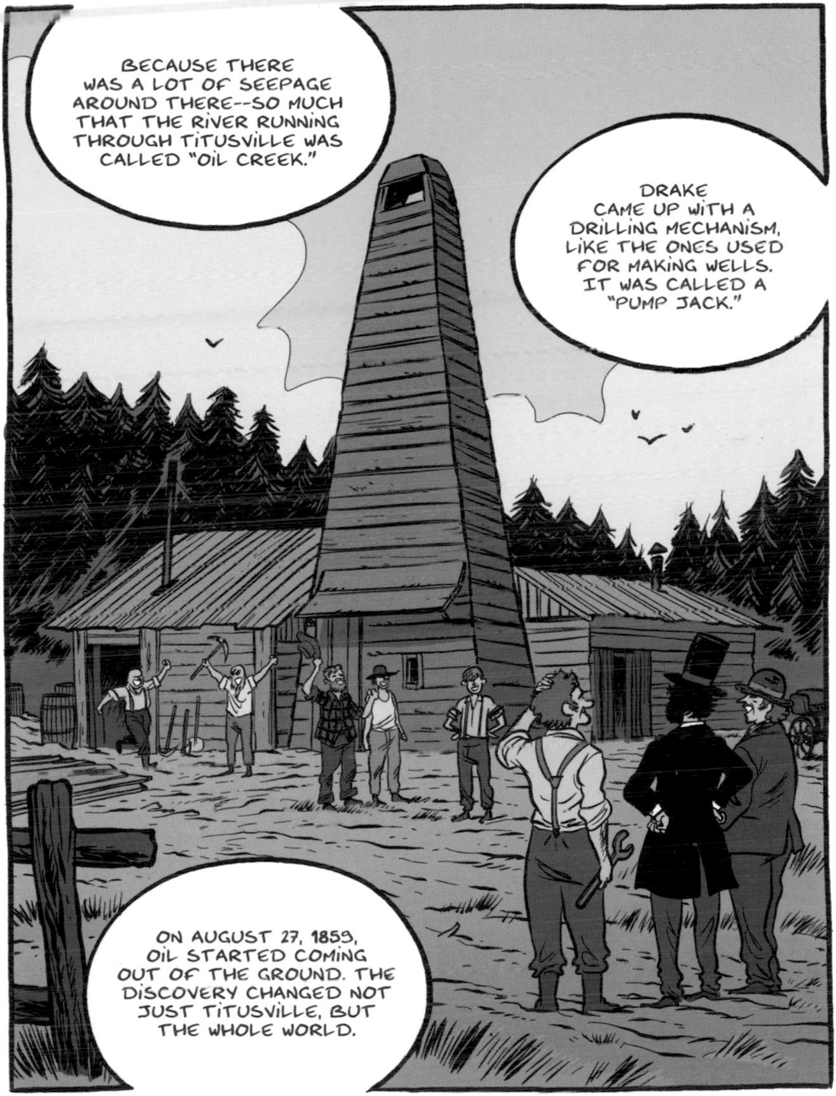
BECAUSE THERE WAS A LOT OF SEEPAGE AROUND THERE--SO MUCH THAT THE RIVER RUNNING THROUGH TITUSVILLE WAS CALLED "OIL CREEK."
DRAKE CAME UP WITH A DRILLING MECHANISM, LIKE THE ONES USED FOR MAKING WELLS. IT WAS CALLED A "PUMP JACK."
ON AUGUST 27, 1859, OIL STARTED COMING OUT OF THE GROUND. THE DISCOVERY CHANGED NOT JUST TITUSVILLE, BUT THE WHOLE WORLD.

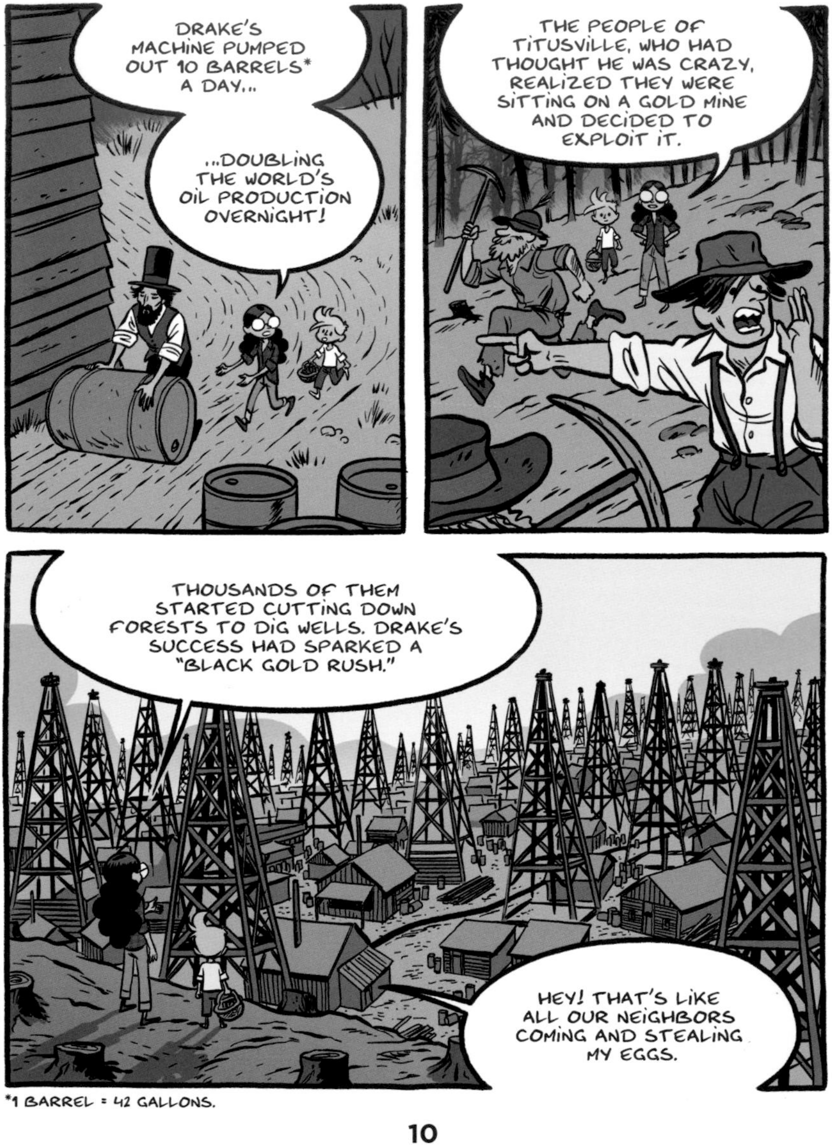
DRAKE'S MACHINE PUMPED OUT 10 BARRELS* A DAY...
...DOUBLING THE WORLD'S OIL PRODUCTION OVERNIGHT!
THE PEOPLE OF TITUSVILLE, WHO HAD THOUGHT HE WAS CRAZY, REALIZED THEY WERE SITTING ON A GOLD MINE AND DECIDED TO EXPLOIT IT.
THOUSANDS OF THEM STARTED CUTTING DOWN FORESTS TO DIG WELLS. DRAKE'S SUCCESS HAD SPARKED A "BLACK GOLD RUSH."
HEY! THAT'S LIKE ALL OUR NEIGHBORS COMING AND STEALING MY EGGS.

*1 BARREL = 42 GALLONS.

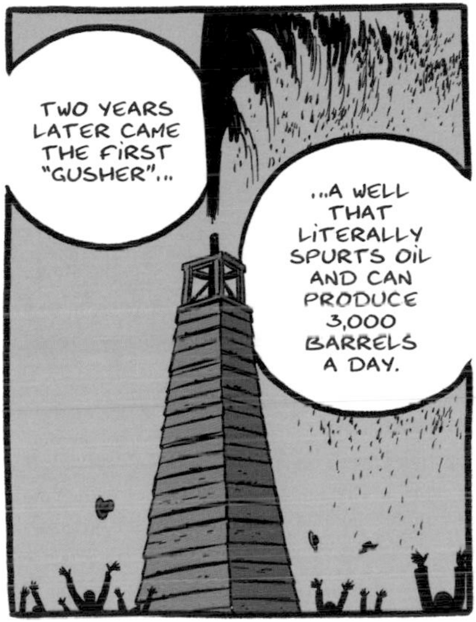
TWO YEARS LATER CAME THE FIRST "GUSHER"...
...A WELL THAT LITERALLY SPURTS OIL AND CAN PRODUCE 3,000 BARRELS A DAY.

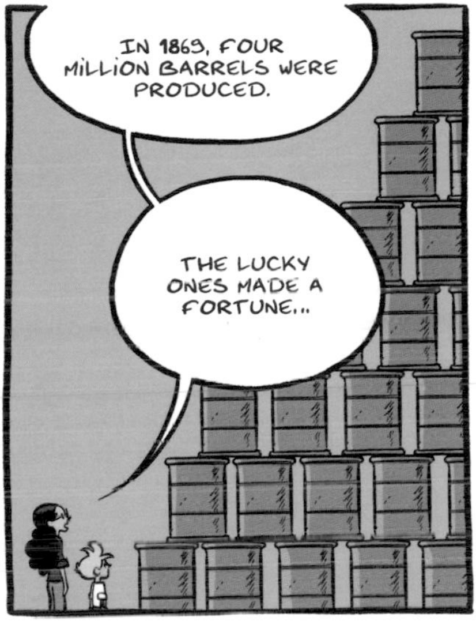
IN 1869, FOUR MILLION BARRELS WERE PRODUCED.
THE LUCKY ONES MADE A FORTUNE...

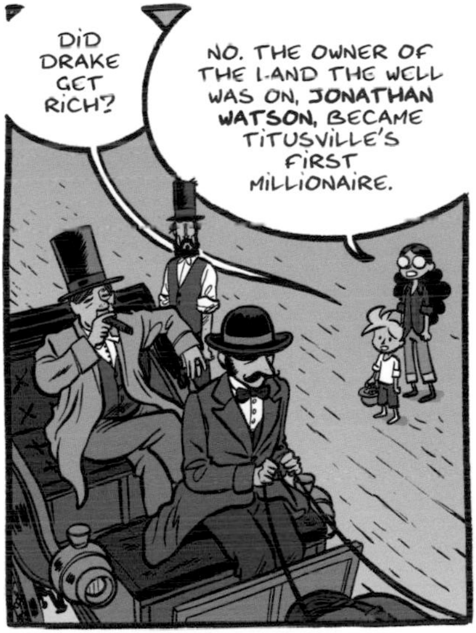
DID DRAKE GET RICH?
NO. THE OWNER OF THE LAND THE WELL WAS ON, **JONATHAN WATSON**, BECAME TITUSVILLE'S FIRST MILLIONAIRE.

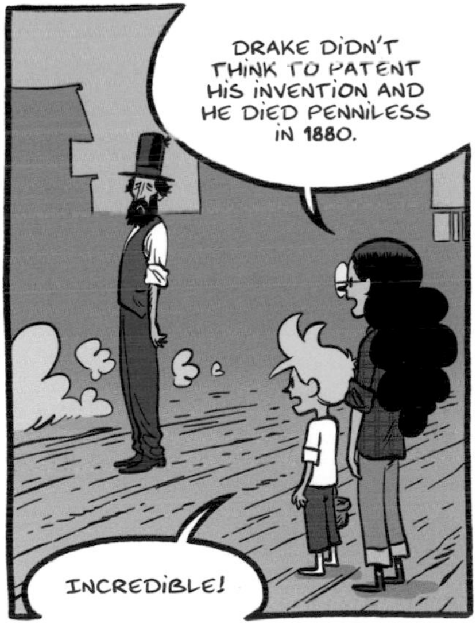
DRAKE DIDN'T THINK TO PATENT HIS INVENTION AND HE DIED PENNILESS IN 1880.
INCREDIBLE!

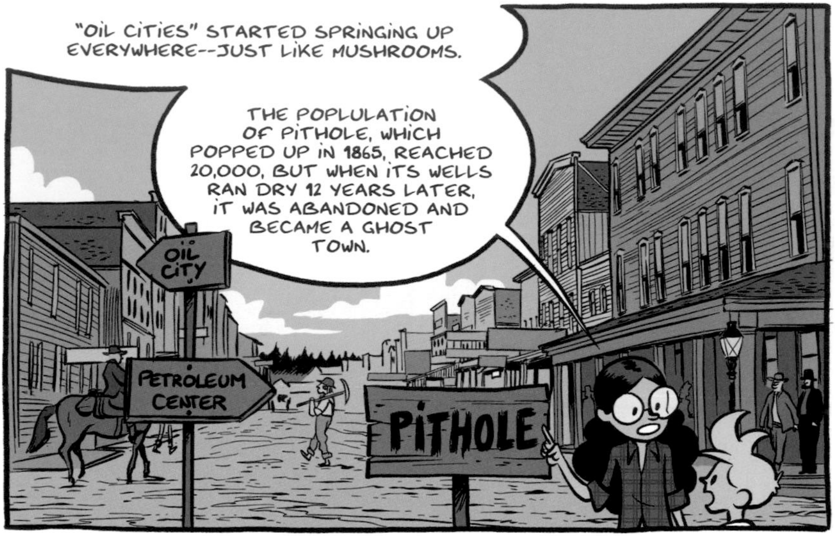
"OIL CITIES" STARTED SPRINGING UP EVERYWHERE--JUST LIKE MUSHROOMS.
THE POPLULATION OF PITHOLE, WHICH POPPED UP IN 1865, REACHED 20,000, BUT WHEN ITS WELLS RAN DRY 12 YEARS LATER, IT WAS ABANDONED AND BECAME A GHOST TOWN.
OIL CITY
PETROLEUM CENTER
PITHOLE

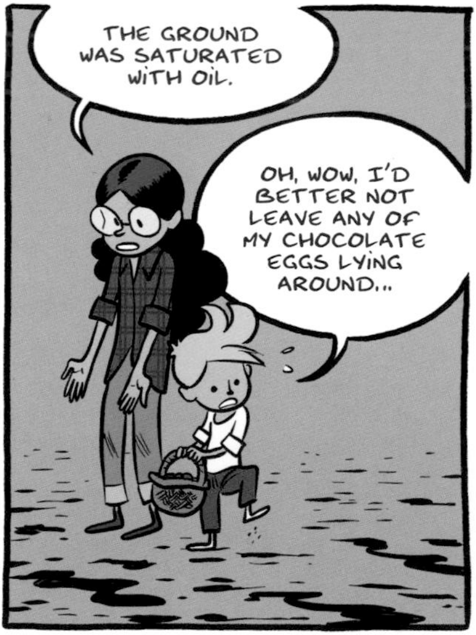
THE GROUND WAS SATURATED WITH OIL.
OH, WOW, I'D BETTER NOT LEAVE ANY OF MY CHOCOLATE EGGS LYING AROUND...

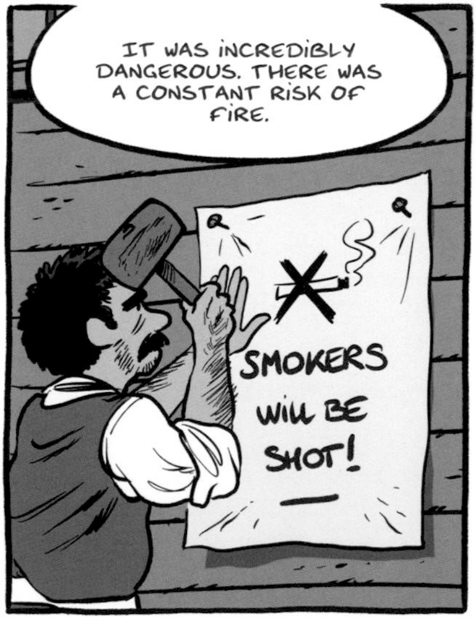
IT WAS INCREDIBLY DANGEROUS. THERE WAS A CONSTANT RISK OF FIRE.
SMOKERS WILL BE SHOT!

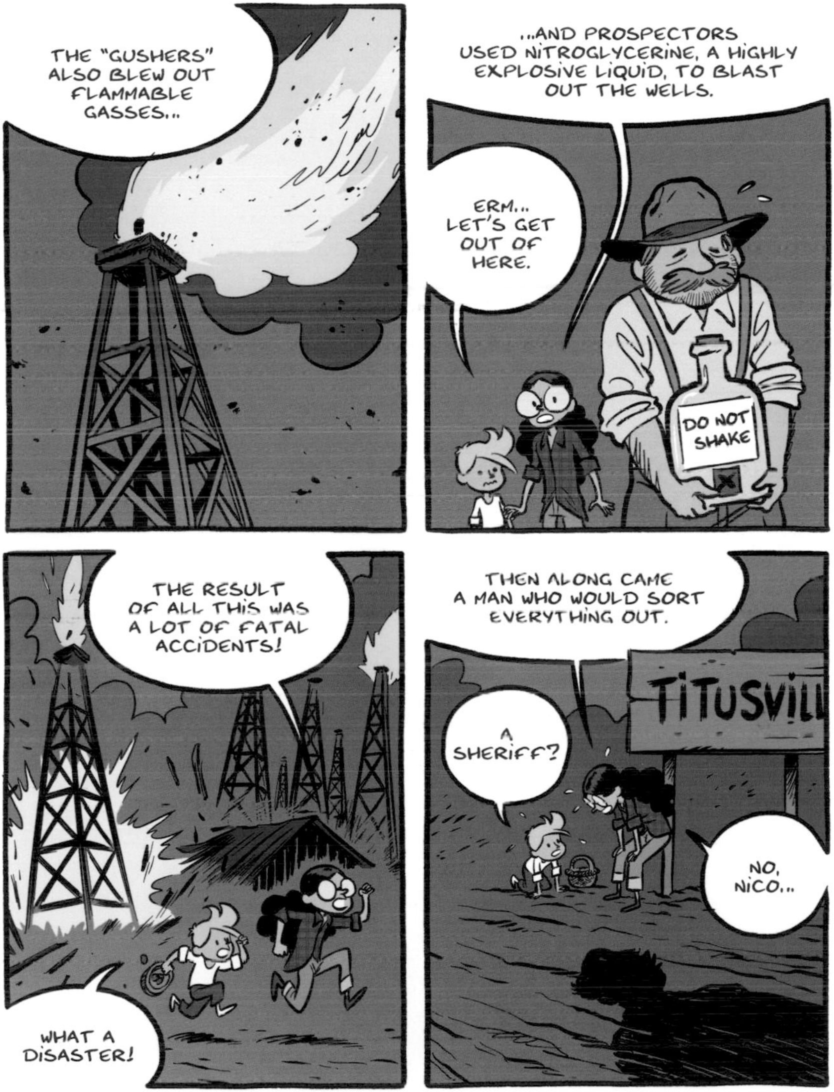
THE "GUSHERS" ALSO BLEW OUT FLAMMABLE GASSES...
...AND PROSPECTORS USED NITROGLYCERINE, A HIGHLY EXPLOSIVE LIQUID, TO BLAST OUT THE WELLS.
ERM... LET'S GET OUT OF HERE.
DO NOT SHAKE
THE RESULT OF ALL THIS WAS A LOT OF FATAL ACCIDENTS!
WHAT A DISASTER!
THEN ALONG CAME A MAN WHO WOULD SORT EVERYTHING OUT.
TITUSVILL
A SHERIFF?
NO, NICO...

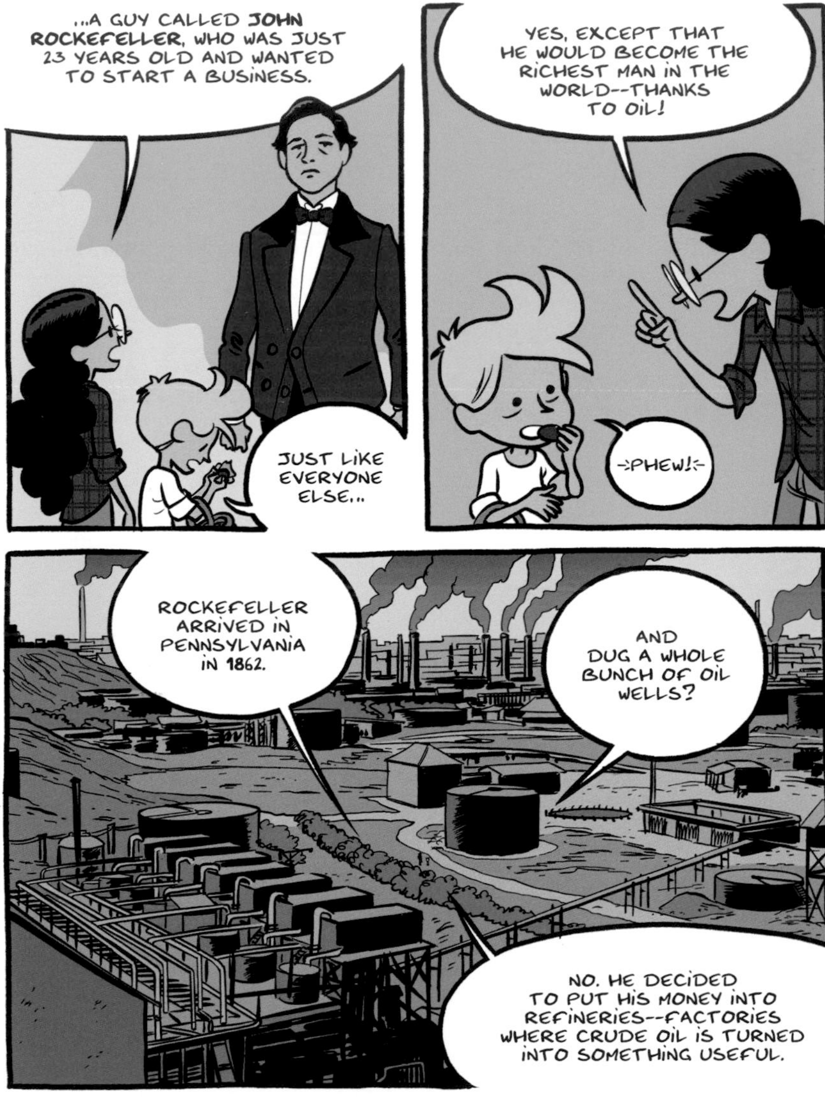
...A GUY CALLED JOHN ROCKEFELLER, WHO WAS JUST 23 YEARS OLD AND WANTED TO START A BUSINESS.
JUST LIKE EVERYONE ELSE...
YES, EXCEPT THAT HE WOULD BECOME THE RICHEST MAN IN THE WORLD--THANKS TO OIL!
PHEW!
ROCKEFELLER ARRIVED IN PENNSYLVANIA IN 1862.
AND DUG A WHOLE BUNCH OF OIL WELLS?
NO. HE DECIDED TO PUT HIS MONEY INTO REFINERIES--FACTORIES WHERE CRUDE OIL IS TURNED INTO SOMETHING USEFUL.

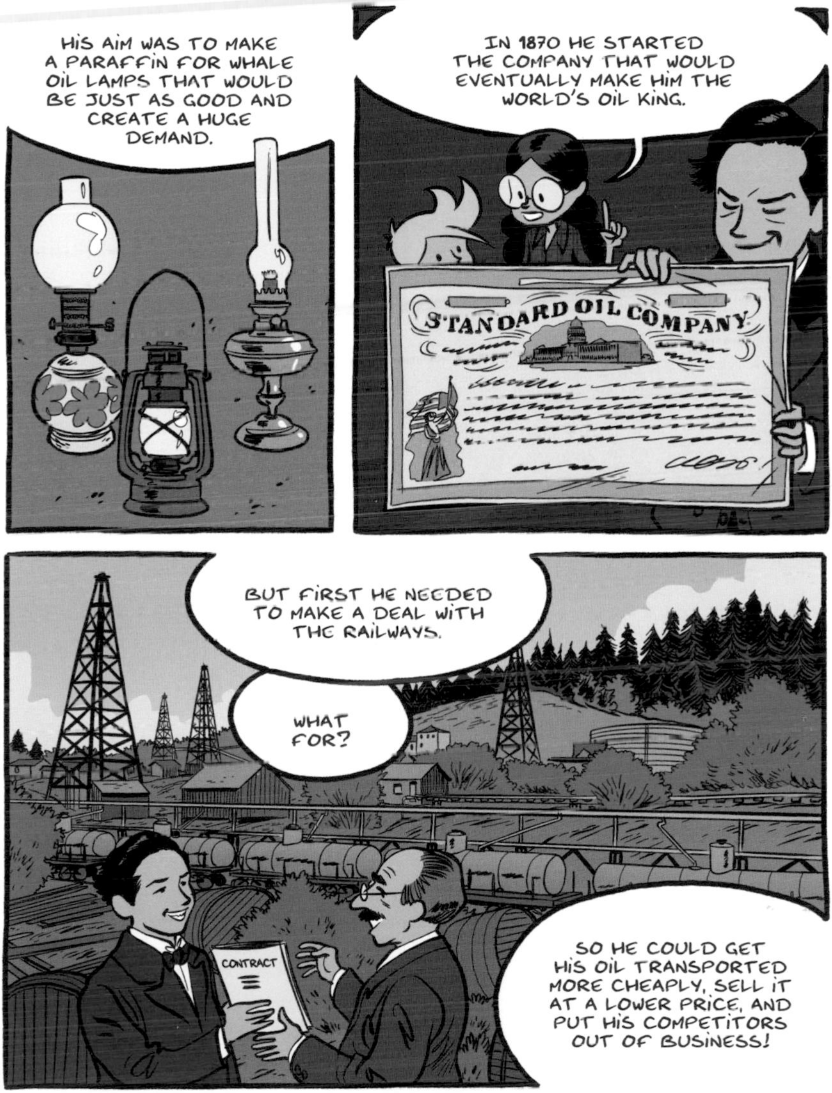

HIS AIM WAS TO MAKE A PARAFFIN FOR WHALE OIL LAMPS THAT WOULD BE JUST AS GOOD AND CREATE A HUGE DEMAND.
IN 1870 HE STARTED THE COMPANY THAT WOULD EVENTUALLY MAKE HIM THE WORLD'S OIL KING.
STANDARD OIL COMPANY
BUT FIRST HE NEEDED TO MAKE A DEAL WITH THE RAILWAYS.
WHAT FOR?
CONTRACT
SO HE COULD GET HIS OIL TRANSPORTED MORE CHEAPLY, SELL IT AT A LOWER PRICE, AND PUT HIS COMPETITORS OUT OF BUSINESS!

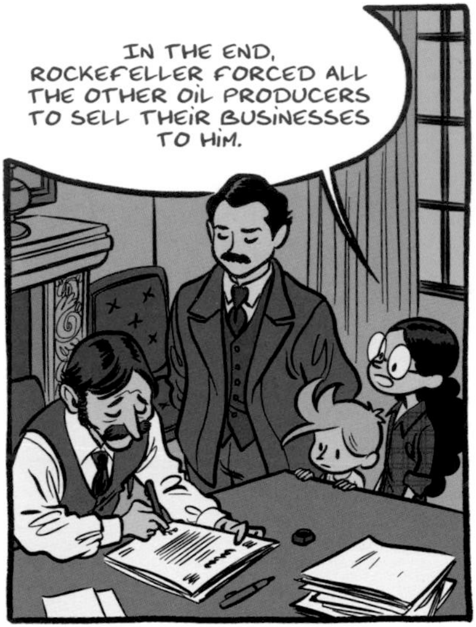
IN THE END, ROCKEFELLER FORCED ALL THE OTHER OIL PRODUCERS TO SELL THEIR BUSINESSES TO HIM.

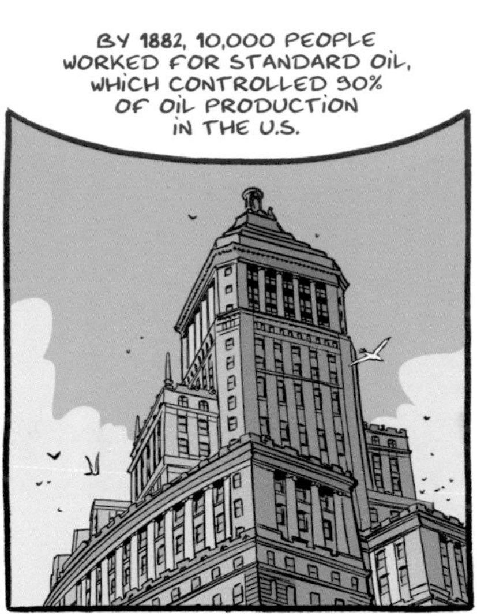
BY 1882, 10,000 PEOPLE WORKED FOR STANDARD OIL, WHICH CONTROLLED 90% OF OIL PRODUCTION IN THE U.S.

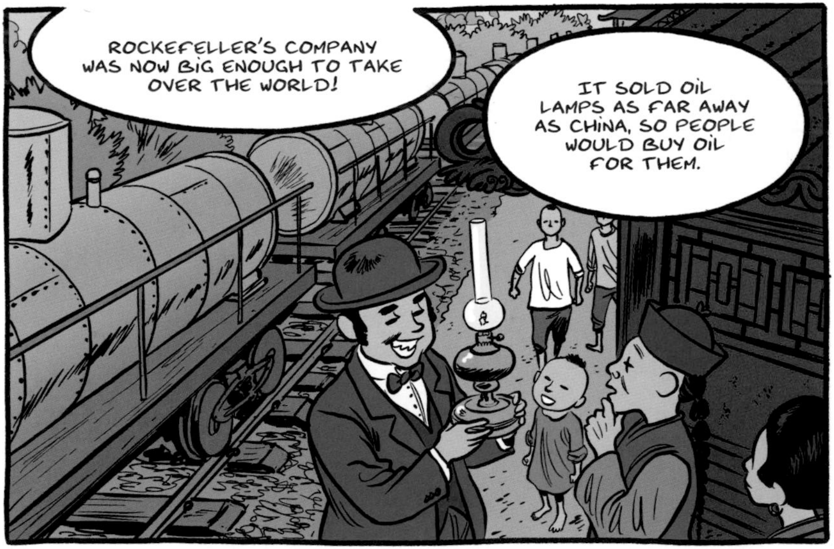
ROCKEFELLER'S COMPANY WAS NOW BIG ENOUGH TO TAKE OVER THE WORLD!
IT SOLD OIL LAMPS AS FAR AWAY AS CHINA, SO PEOPLE WOULD BUY OIL FOR THEM.

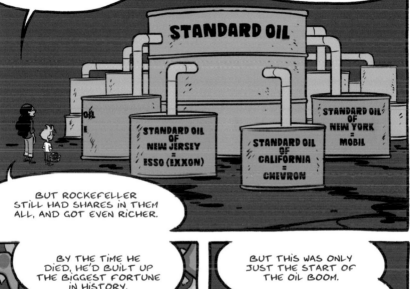

STANDARD OIL BECAME SO POWERFUL THAT PEOPLE BEGAN TO WORRY...

...AND IN 1911, THE GOVERNMENT MADE IT SPLIT INTO 34 SEPARATE FIRMS.*

STANDARD OIL

STANDARD OIL OF NEW JERSEY = ESSO (EXXON)

STANDARD OIL OF CALIFORNIA = CHEVRON

STANDARD OIL OF NEW YORK = MOBIL

BUT ROCKEFELLER STILL HAD SHARES IN THEM ALL, AND GOT EVEN RICHER.

BY THE TIME HE DIED, HE'D BUILT UP THE BIGGEST FORTUNE IN HISTORY.

BUT THIS WAS ONLY JUST THE START OF THE OIL BOOM.

THERE WERE STILL MASSIVE RESERVES TO DISCOVER...

*FOLLOWING THE SHERMAN ANTITRUST ACT OF 1890 WHICH LIMITED THE SIZE OF COMPANIES.

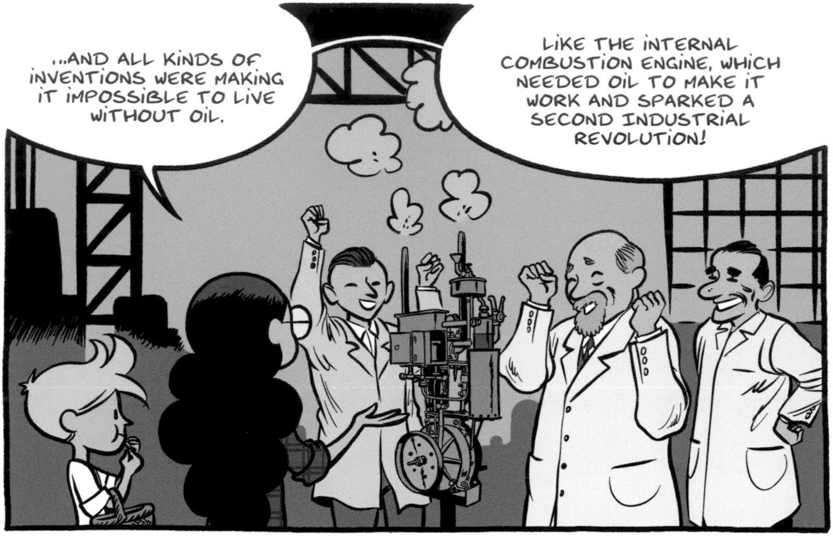
...AND ALL KINDS OF INVENTIONS WERE MAKING IT IMPOSSIBLE TO LIVE WITHOUT OIL.
LIKE THE INTERNAL COMBUSTION ENGINE, WHICH NEEDED OIL TO MAKE IT WORK AND SPARKED A SECOND INDUSTRIAL REVOLUTION!

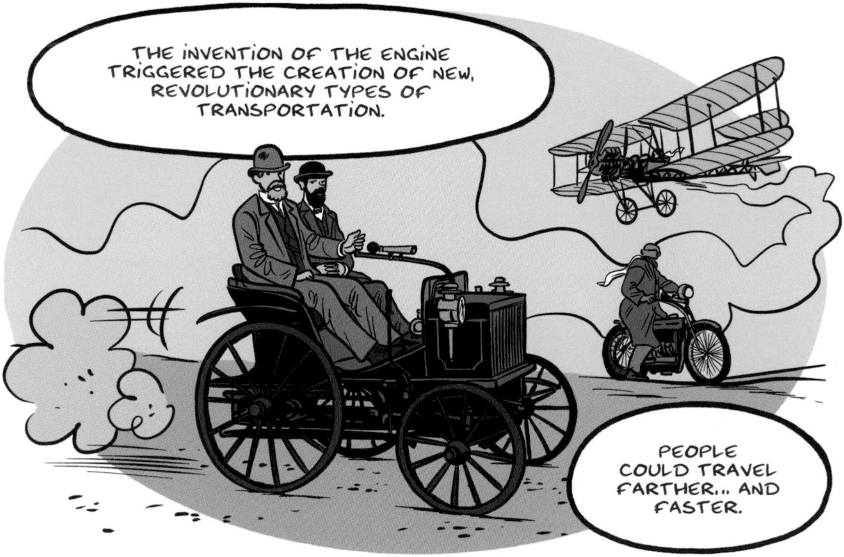
THE INVENTION OF THE ENGINE TRIGGERED THE CREATION OF NEW, REVOLUTIONARY TYPES OF TRANSPORTATION.
PEOPLE COULD TRAVEL FARTHER... AND FASTER.

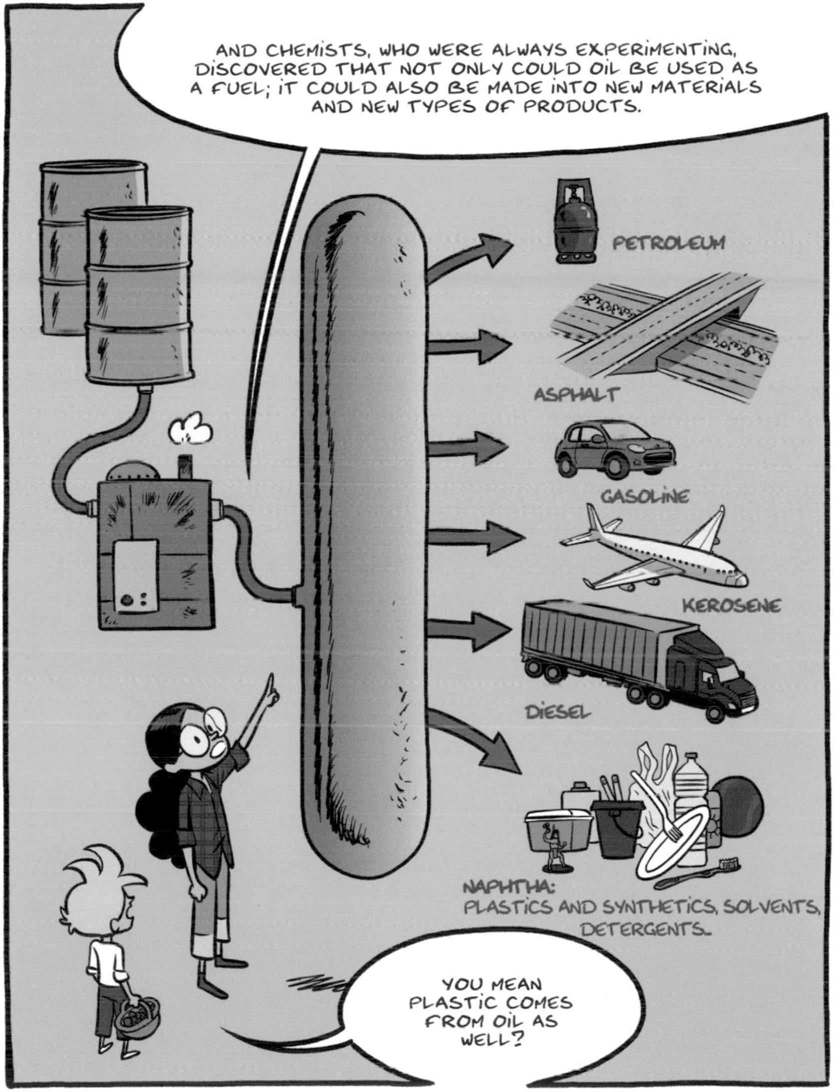
AND CHEMISTS, WHO WERE ALWAYS EXPERIMENTING, DISCOVERED THAT NOT ONLY COULD OIL BE USED AS A FUEL; IT COULD ALSO BE MADE INTO NEW MATERIALS AND NEW TYPES OF PRODUCTS.
PETROLEUM
ASPHALT
GASOLINE
KEROSENE
DIESEL
NAPHTHA:
PLASTICS AND SYNTHETICS, SOLVENTS, DETERGENTS...
YOU MEAN PLASTIC COMES FROM OIL AS WELL?

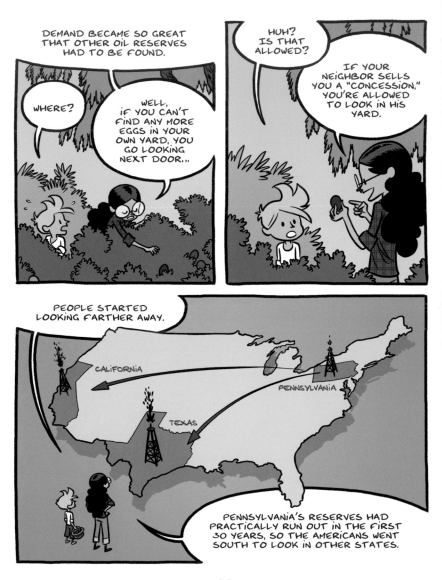

DEMAND BECAME SO GREAT THAT OTHER OIL RESERVES HAD TO BE FOUND.

WHERE?

WELL, IF YOU CAN'T FIND ANY MORE EGGS IN YOUR OWN YARD, YOU GO LOOKING NEXT DOOR...

HUH? IS THAT ALLOWED?

IF YOUR NEIGHBOR SELLS YOU A "CONCESSION," YOU'RE ALLOWED TO LOOK IN HIS YARD.

PEOPLE STARTED LOOKING FARTHER AWAY.

CALIFORNIA

PENNSYLVANIA

TEXAS

PENNSYLVANIA'S RESERVES HAD PRACTICALLY RUN OUT IN THE FIRST 30 YEARS, SO THE AMERICANS WENT SOUTH TO LOOK IN OTHER STATES.

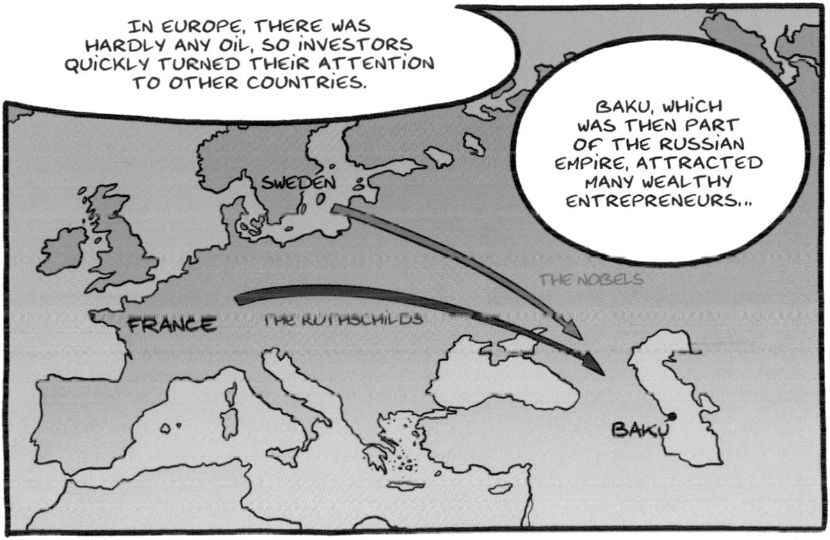
IN EUROPE, THERE WAS HARDLY ANY OIL, SO INVESTORS QUICKLY TURNED THEIR ATTENTION TO OTHER COUNTRIES.
BAKU, WHICH WAS THEN PART OF THE RUSSIAN EMPIRE, ATTRACTED MANY WEALTHY ENTREPRENEURS...
SWEDEN
THE NOBELS
FRANCE
THE ROTHSCHILDS
BAKU

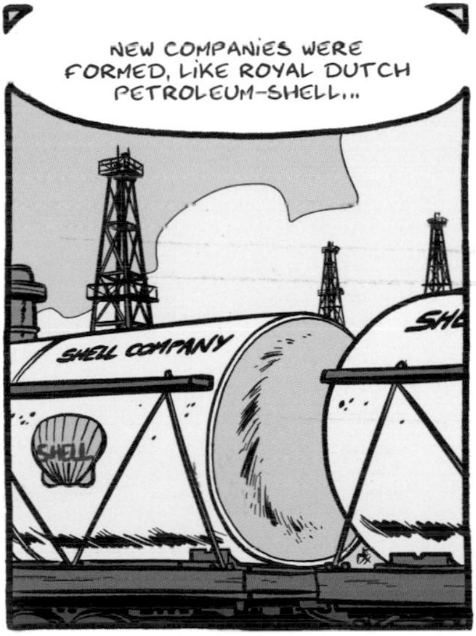
NEW COMPANIES WERE FORMED, LIKE ROYAL DUTCH PETROLEUM-SHELL...
SHELL COMPANY
SHELL

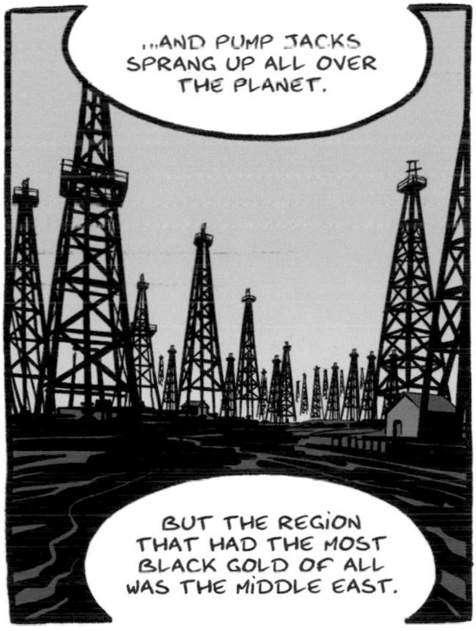
...AND PUMP JACKS SPRANG UP ALL OVER THE PLANET.
BUT THE REGION THAT HAD THE MOST BLACK GOLD OF ALL WAS THE MIDDLE EAST.

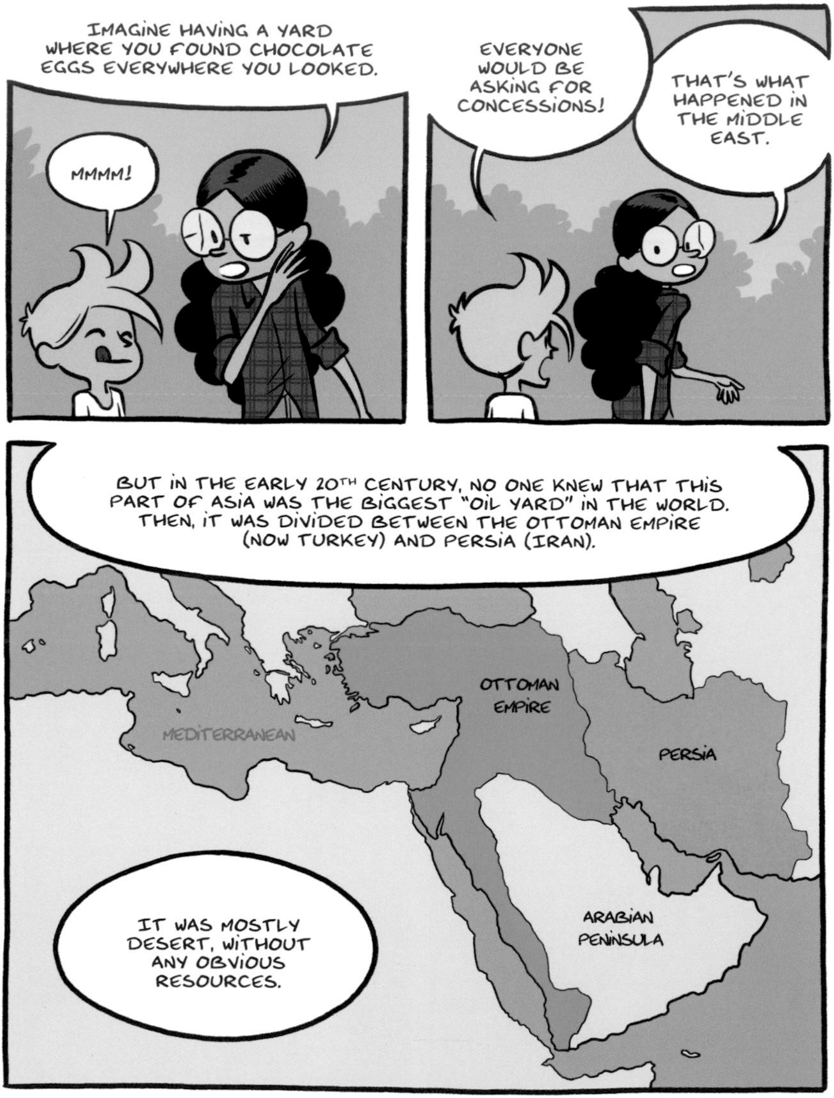
IMAGINE HAVING A YARD WHERE YOU FOUND CHOCOLATE EGGS EVERYWHERE YOU LOOKED.
MMMM!
EVERYONE WOULD BE ASKING FOR CONCESSIONS!
THAT'S WHAT HAPPENED IN THE MIDDLE EAST.
BUT IN THE EARLY 20TH CENTURY, NO ONE KNEW THAT THIS PART OF ASIA WAS THE BIGGEST "OIL YARD" IN THE WORLD. THEN, IT WAS DIVIDED BETWEEN THE OTTOMAN EMPIRE (NOW TURKEY) AND PERSIA (IRAN).
OTTOMAN EMPIRE
MEDITERRANEAN
PERSIA
ARABIAN PENINSULA
IT WAS MOSTLY DESERT, WITHOUT ANY OBVIOUS RESOURCES.

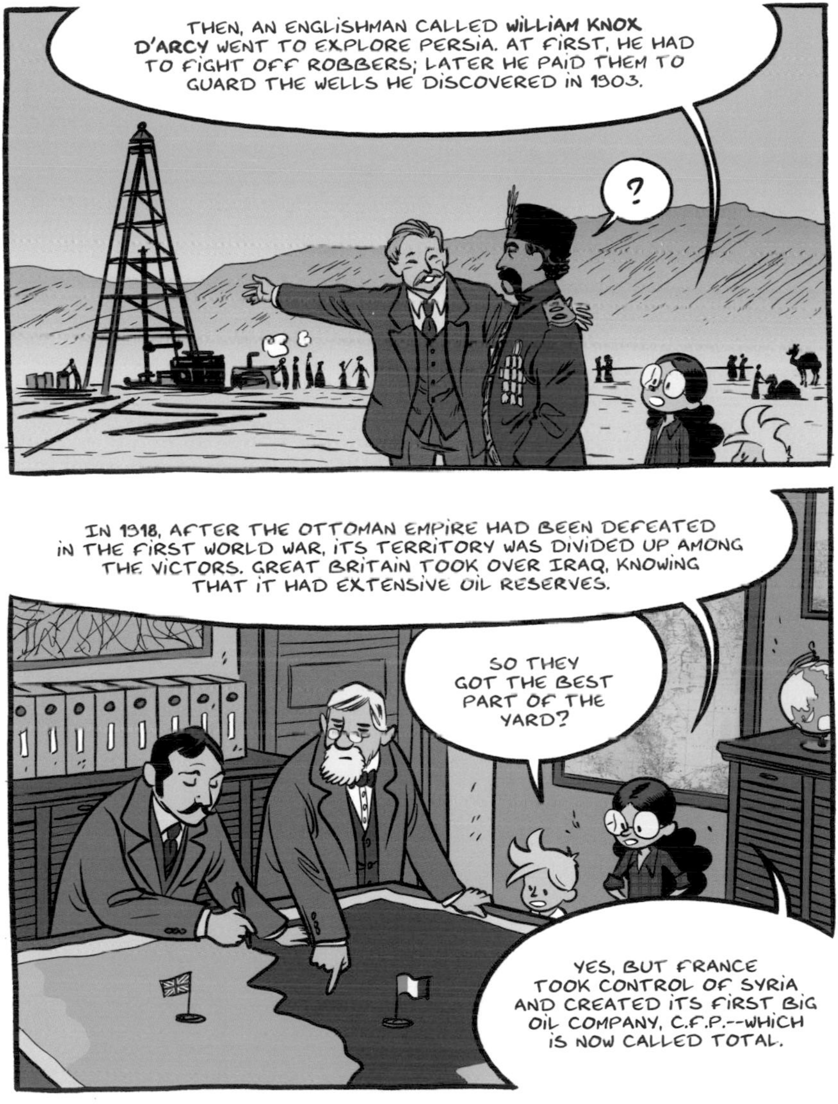
THEN, AN ENGLISHMAN CALLED WILLIAM KNOX D'ARCY WENT TO EXPLORE PERSIA. AT FIRST, HE HAD TO FIGHT OFF ROBBERS; LATER HE PAID THEM TO GUARD THE WELLS HE DISCOVERED IN 1903.
?
IN 1918, AFTER THE OTTOMAN EMPIRE HAD BEEN DEFEATED IN THE FIRST WORLD WAR, ITS TERRITORY WAS DIVIDED UP AMONG THE VICTORS. GREAT BRITAIN TOOK OVER IRAQ, KNOWING THAT IT HAD EXTENSIVE OIL RESERVES.
SO THEY GOT THE BEST PART OF THE YARD?
YES, BUT FRANCE TOOK CONTROL OF SYRIA AND CREATED ITS FIRST BIG OIL COMPANY, C.F.P.--WHICH IS NOW CALLED TOTAL.

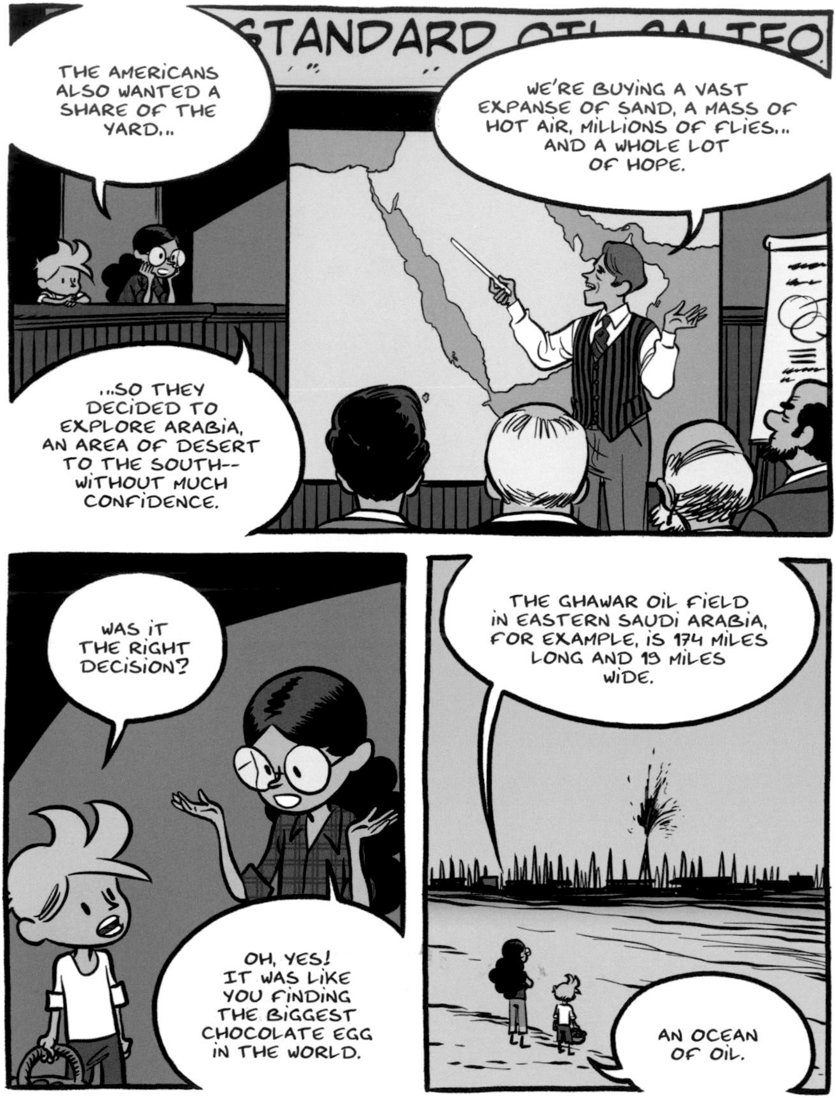
STANDARD OIL
THE AMERICANS ALSO WANTED A SHARE OF THE YARD...
WE'RE BUYING A VAST EXPANSE OF SAND, A MASS OF HOT AIR, MILLIONS OF FLIES... AND A WHOLE LOT OF HOPE.
...SO THEY DECIDED TO EXPLORE ARABIA, AN AREA OF DESERT TO THE SOUTH-- WITHOUT MUCH CONFIDENCE.
WAS IT THE RIGHT DECISION?
OH, YES! IT WAS LIKE YOU FINDING THE BIGGEST CHOCOLATE EGG IN THE WORLD.
THE GHAWAR OIL FIELD IN EASTERN SAUDI ARABIA, FOR EXAMPLE, IS 174 MILES LONG AND 19 MILES WIDE.
AN OCEAN OF OIL.

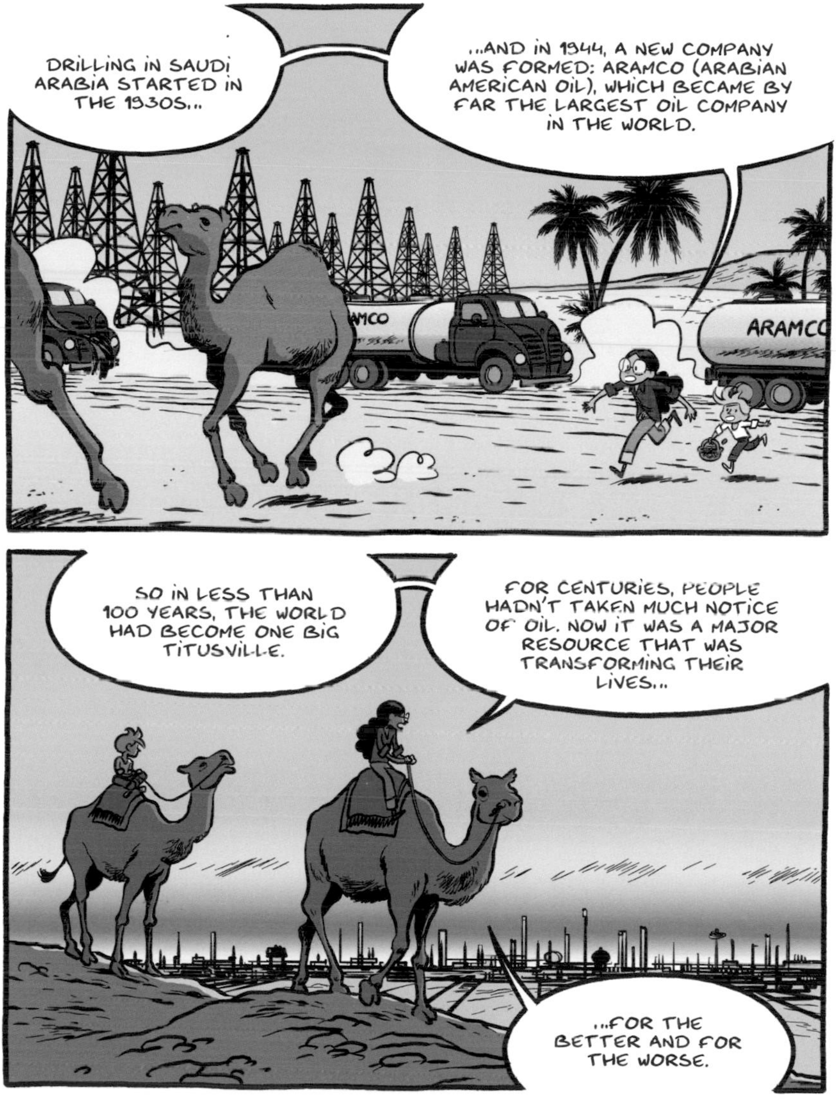
DRILLING IN SAUDI ARABIA STARTED IN THE 1930S...
...AND IN 1944, A NEW COMPANY WAS FORMED: ARAMCO (ARABIAN AMERICAN OIL), WHICH BECAME BY FAR THE LARGEST OIL COMPANY IN THE WORLD.
ARAMCO
SO IN LESS THAN 100 YEARS, THE WORLD HAD BECOME ONE BIG TITUSVILLE.
FOR CENTURIES, PEOPLE HADN'T TAKEN MUCH NOTICE OF OIL. NOW IT WAS A MAJOR RESOURCE THAT WAS TRANSFORMING THEIR LIVES...
...FOR THE BETTER AND FOR THE WORSE.

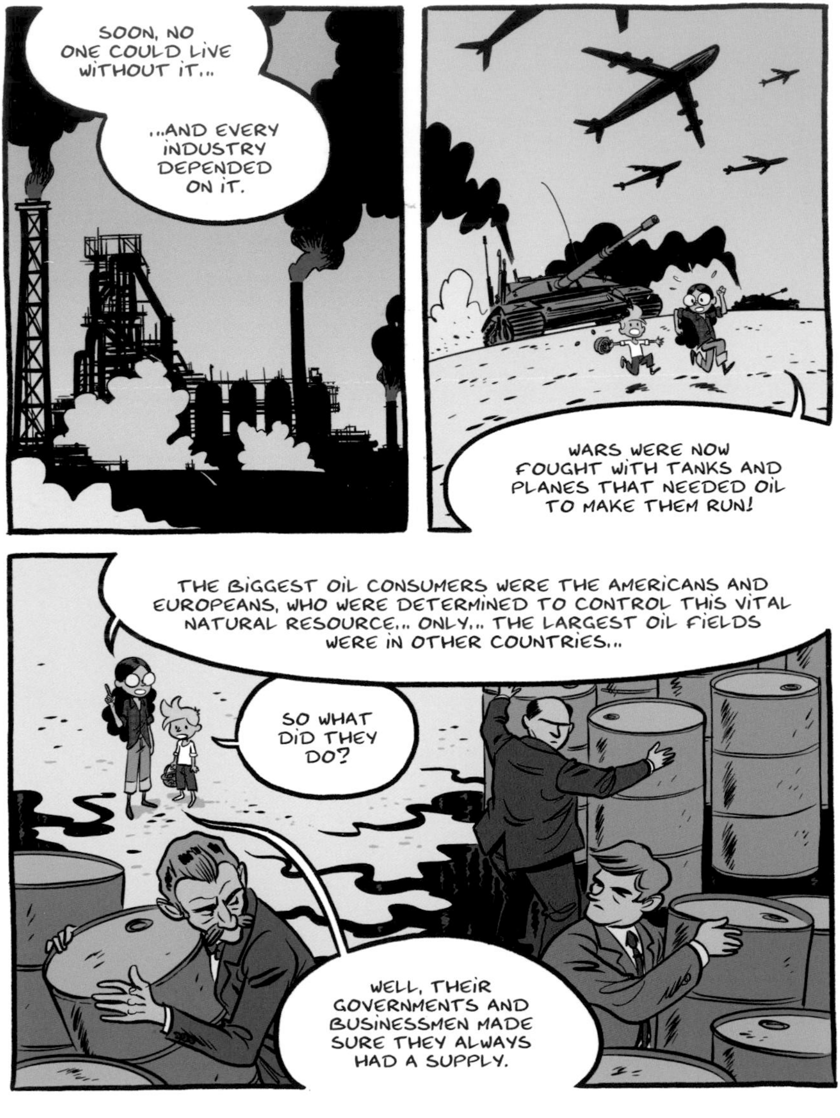
SOON, NO ONE COULD LIVE WITHOUT IT...
...AND EVERY INDUSTRY DEPENDED ON IT.
WARS WERE NOW FOUGHT WITH TANKS AND PLANES THAT NEEDED OIL TO MAKE THEM RUN!
THE BIGGEST OIL CONSUMERS WERE THE AMERICANS AND EUROPEANS, WHO WERE DETERMINED TO CONTROL THIS VITAL NATURAL RESOURCE... ONLY... THE LARGEST OIL FIELDS WERE IN OTHER COUNTRIES...
SO WHAT DID THEY DO?
WELL, THEIR GOVERNMENTS AND BUSINESSMEN MADE SURE THEY ALWAYS HAD A SUPPLY.

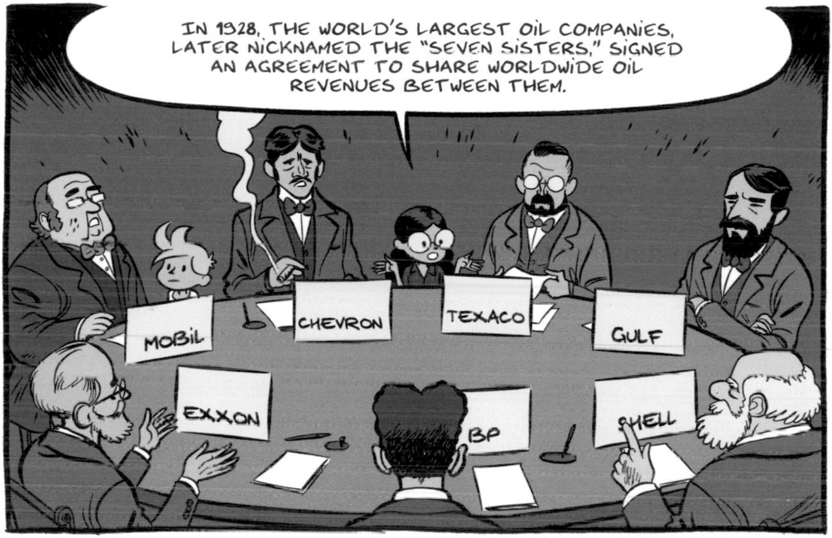
IN 1928, THE WORLD'S LARGEST OIL COMPANIES, LATER NICKNAMED THE "SEVEN SISTERS," SIGNED AN AGREEMENT TO SHARE WORLDWIDE OIL REVENUES BETWEEN THEM.
MOBIL
CHEVRON
TEXACO
GULF
EXXON
BP
SHELL

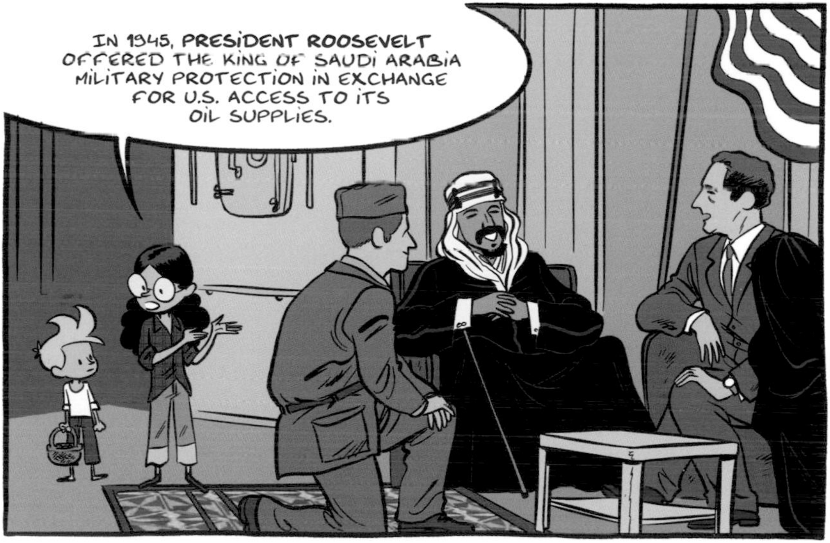
IN 1945, PRESIDENT ROOSEVELT OFFERED THE KING OF SAUDI ARABIA MILITARY PROTECTION IN EXCHANGE FOR U.S. ACCESS TO ITS OIL SUPPLIES.

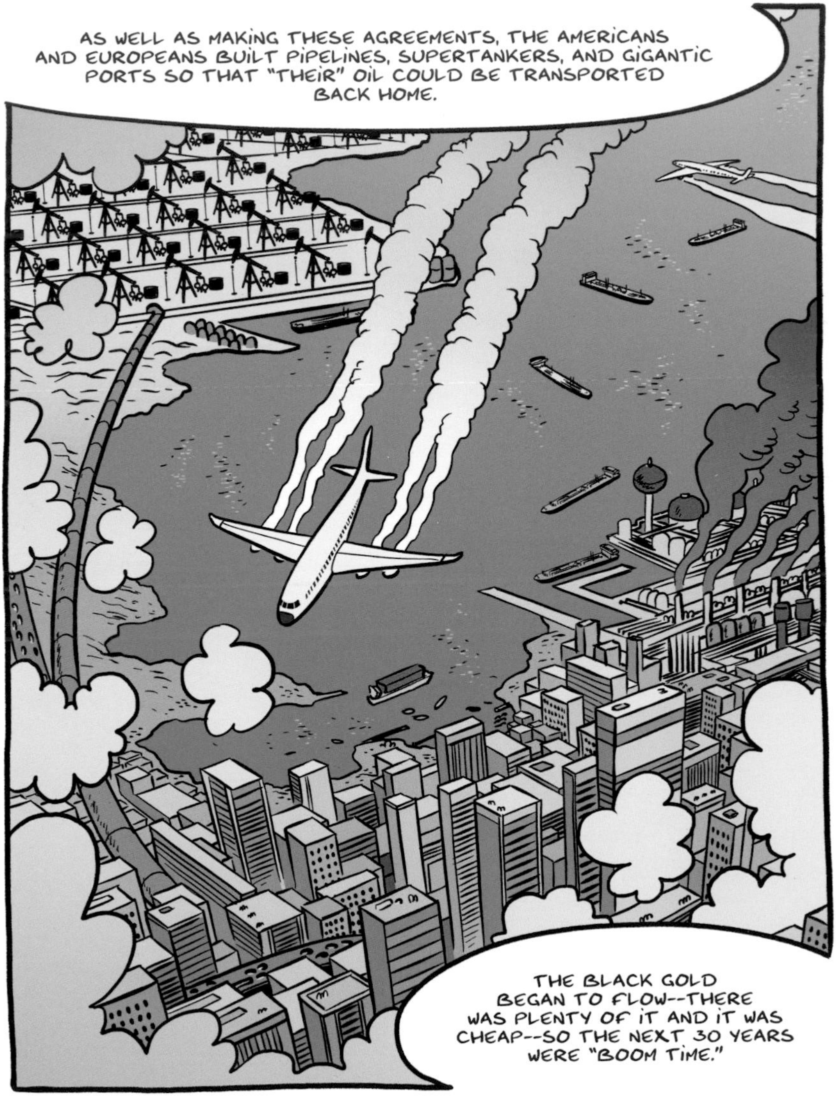
AS WELL AS MAKING THESE AGREEMENTS, THE AMERICANS AND EUROPEANS BUILT PIPELINES, SUPERTANKERS, AND GIGANTIC PORTS SO THAT "THEIR" OIL COULD BE TRANSPORTED BACK HOME.
THE BLACK GOLD BEGAN TO FLOW--THERE WAS PLENTY OF IT AND IT WAS CHEAP--SO THE NEXT 30 YEARS WERE "BOOM TIME."

AND THE MIDDLE EASTERN COUNTRIES WHERE THE OIL WAS, DID THEY GET RICH, TOO?
HARDLY AT ALL, BECAUSE THE SUPPLIES WERE UNDER FOREIGN CONTROL.
SO THEY HAD EGGS IN THEIR YARD, BUT THEY WEREN'T ALLOWED TO EAT THEM?
RIGHT, AND THE CONCESSIONS LASTED A LONG TIME.
A FEW LEADERS GOT RICH, BUT THE PEOPLE BARELY SAW ANY OF THE PROFITS...
THEY MISSED OUT ON ALL THE MONEY, LIKE DRAKE!
IT WAS A TENSE SITUATION THAT RESULTED IN CONFLICT IN THE SECOND HALF OF THE 20TH CENTURY.
OOPS...

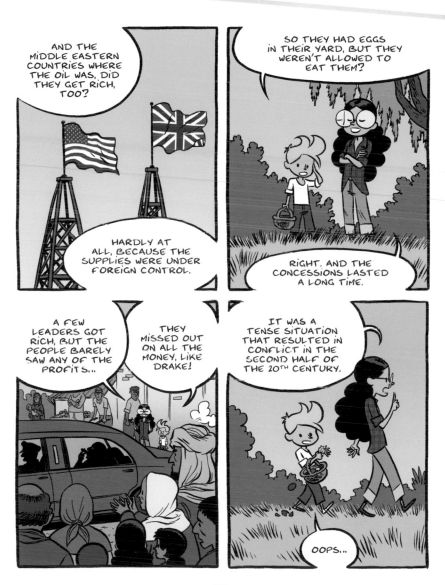

IN IRAN (THE NEW NAME FOR PERSIA), WHERE THE BRITISH CONTROLLED THE OIL SUPPLY, **PRIME MINISTER MOSADDEGH** DECIDED TO NATIONALIZE IT SO THAT HIS PEOPLE COULD BENEFIT.

OUCH! I BET THAT DIDN'T MAKE THE OIL COMPANIES HAPPY.

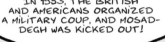

IN 1953, THE BRITISH AND AMERICANS ORGANIZED A MILITARY COUP, AND MOSADDEGH WAS KICKED OUT!

IN 1960, THE OIL-PRODUCING COUNTRIES FORMED AN ORGANIZATION CALLED **O.P.E.C.** IN ORDER TO CONTROL THE PRICE OF OIL, WHICH THE FOREIGN COMPANIES HAD PREVIOUSLY FIXED.

*THE ORGANIZATION OF THE PETROLEUM EXPORTING COUNTRIES.

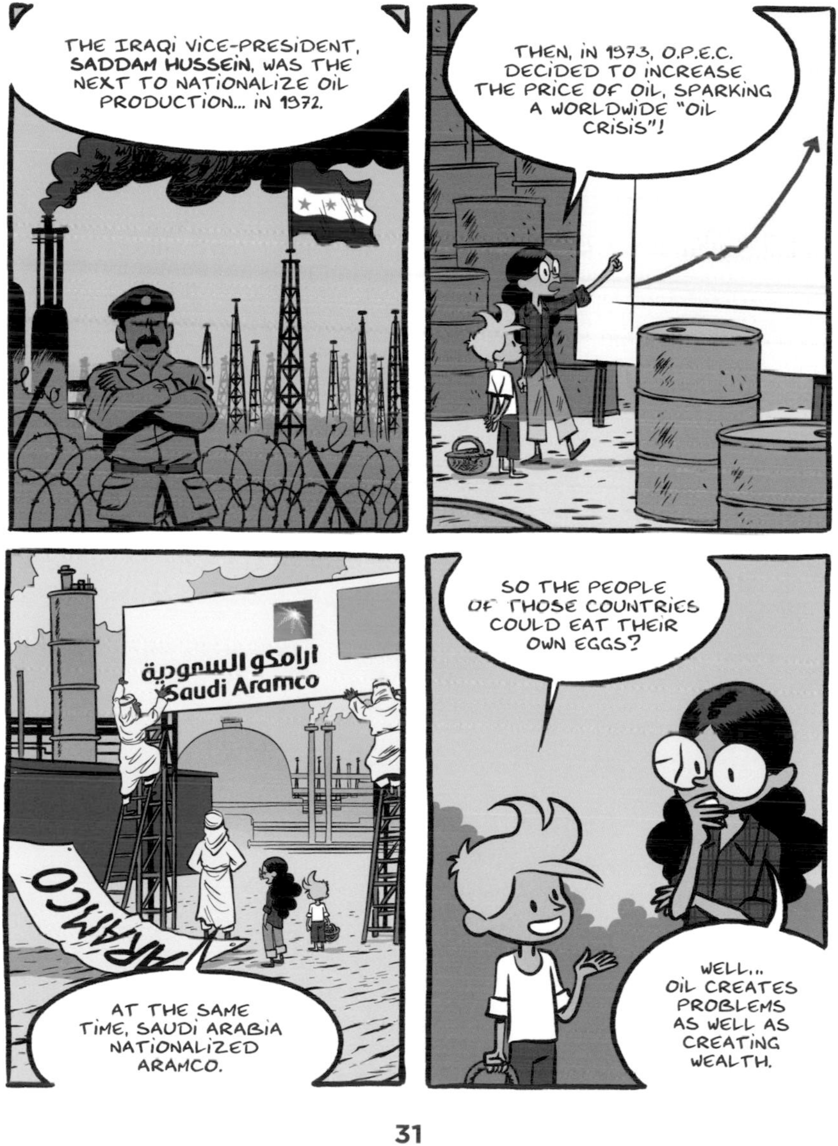

THE IRAQI VICE-PRESIDENT, **SADDAM HUSSEIN**, WAS THE NEXT TO NATIONALIZE OIL PRODUCTION... IN 1972.
THEN, IN 1973, O.P.E.C. DECIDED TO INCREASE THE PRICE OF OIL, SPARKING A WORLDWIDE "OIL CRISIS"!
ارامكو السعودية
Saudi Aramco
ARAMCO
AT THE SAME TIME, SAUDI ARABIA NATIONALIZED ARAMCO.
SO THE PEOPLE OF THOSE COUNTRIES COULD EAT THEIR OWN EGGS?
WELL... OIL CREATES PROBLEMS AS WELL AS CREATING WEALTH.

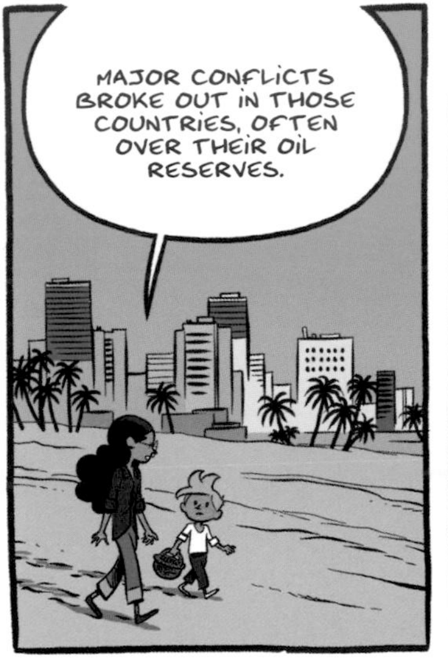
MAJOR CONFLICTS BROKE OUT IN THOSE COUNTRIES, OFTEN OVER THEIR OIL RESERVES.

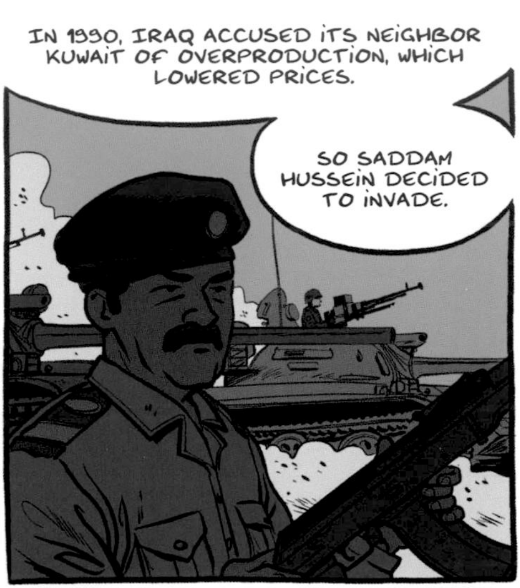
IN 1990, IRAQ ACCUSED ITS NEIGHBOR KUWAIT OF OVERPRODUCTION, WHICH LOWERED PRICES.
SO SADDAM HUSSEIN DECIDED TO INVADE.

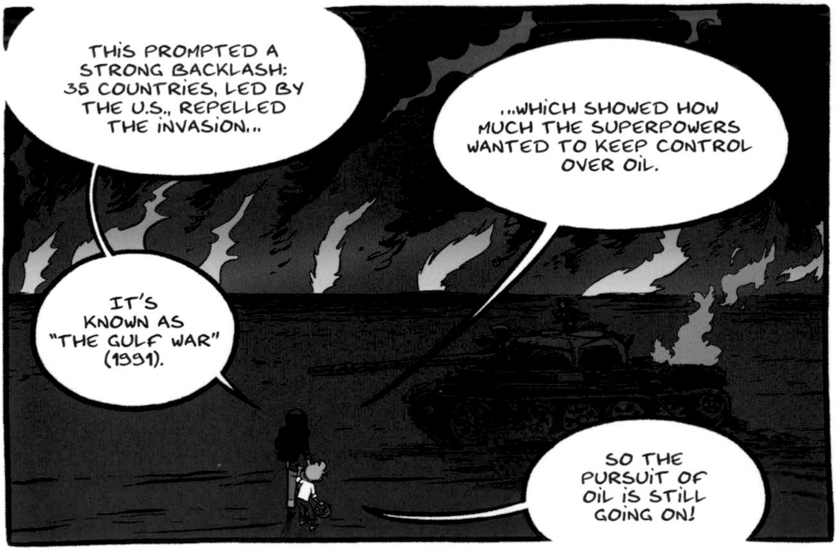
THIS PROMPTED A STRONG BACKLASH: 35 COUNTRIES, LED BY THE U.S., REPELLED THE INVASION...
...WHICH SHOWED HOW MUCH THE SUPERPOWERS WANTED TO KEEP CONTROL OVER OIL.
IT'S KNOWN AS "THE GULF WAR" (1991).
SO THE PURSUIT OF OIL IS STILL GOING ON!

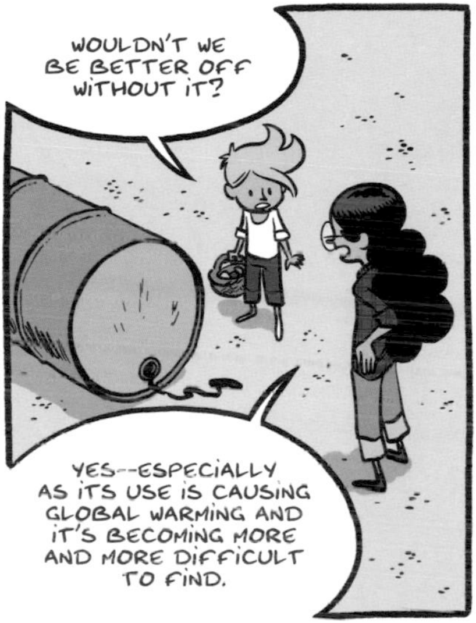
WOULDN'T WE BE BETTER OFF WITHOUT IT?
YES--ESPECIALLY AS ITS USE IS CAUSING GLOBAL WARMING AND IT'S BECOMING MORE AND MORE DIFFICULT TO FIND.

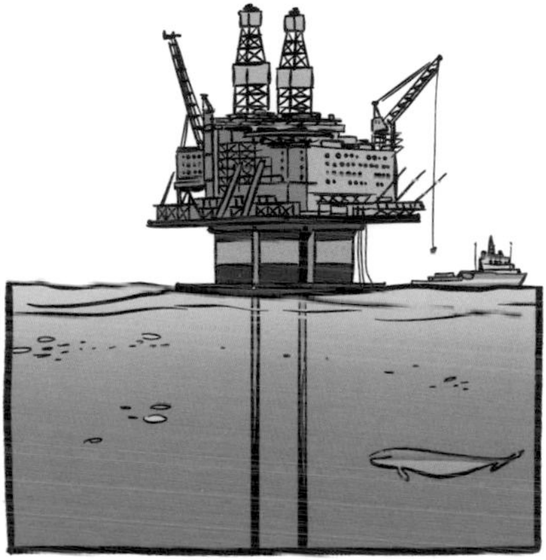
DRAKE FOUND OIL 70 FEET UNDERGROUND. TODAY, WE HAVE TO DRILL SIX MILES BENEATH THE SEABED TO GET TO IT.

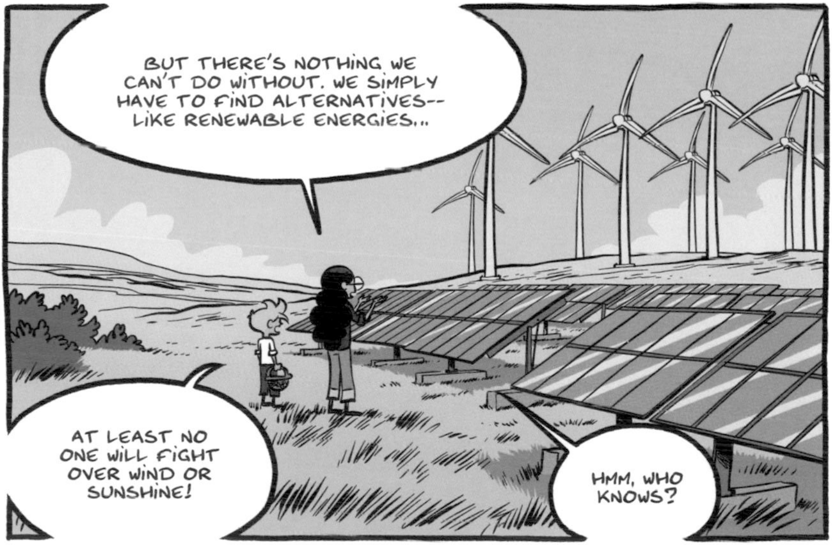
BUT THERE'S NOTHING WE CAN'T DO WITHOUT. WE SIMPLY HAVE TO FIND ALTERNATIVES--LIKE RENEWABLE ENERGIES...
AT LEAST NO ONE WILL FIGHT OVER WIND OR SUNSHINE!
HMM, WHO KNOWS?

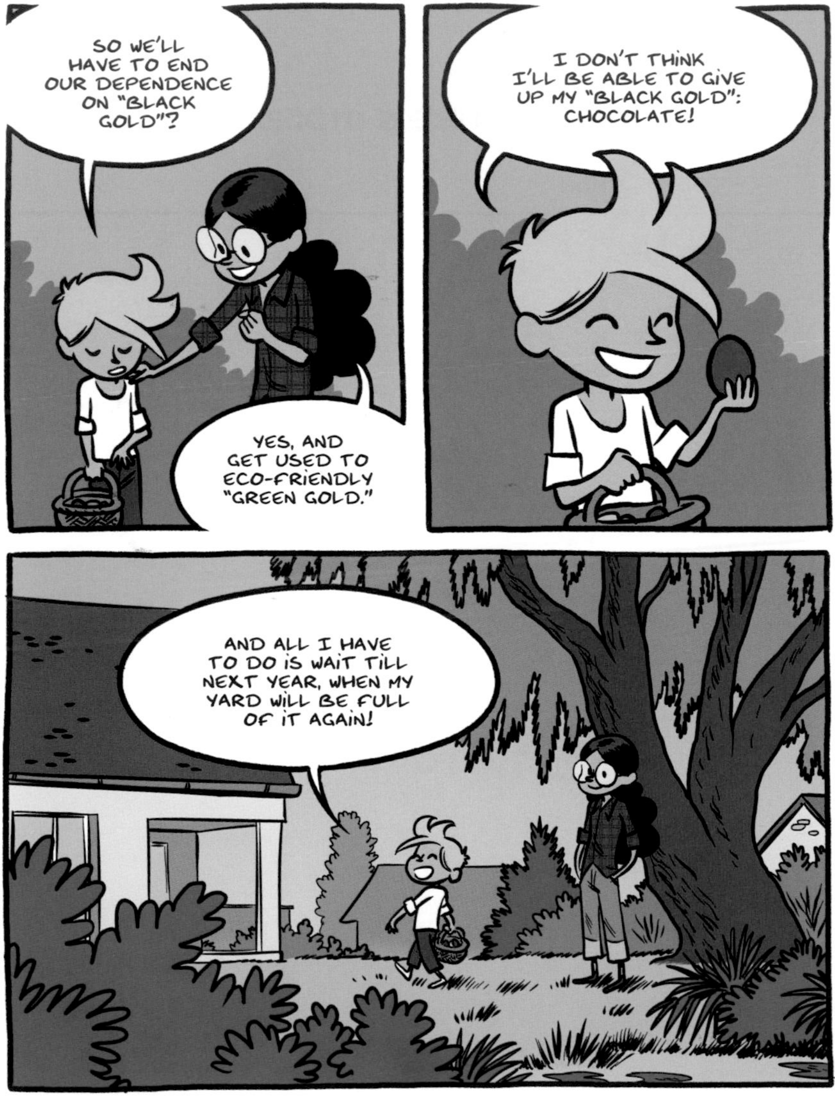
SO WE'LL HAVE TO END OUR DEPENDENCE ON "BLACK GOLD"?
YES, AND GET USED TO ECO-FRIENDLY "GREEN GOLD."
I DON'T THINK I'LL BE ABLE TO GIVE UP MY "BLACK GOLD": CHOCOLATE!
AND ALL I HAVE TO DO IS WAIT TILL NEXT YEAR, WHEN MY YARD WILL BE FULL OF IT AGAIN!

And there's more...

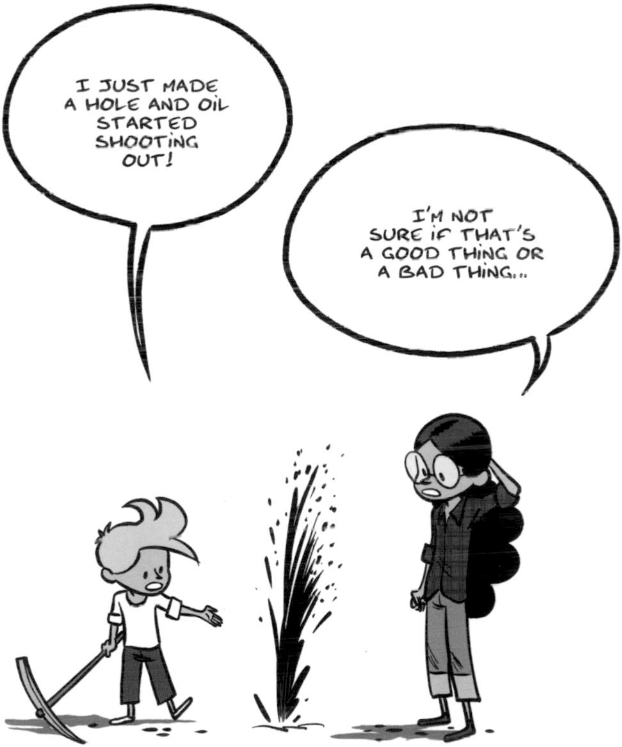
I JUST MADE A HOLE AND OIL STARTED SHOOTING OUT!
I'M NOT SURE IF THAT'S A GOOD THING OR A BAD THING...

Some people who made history

John D. Rockefeller
(1839-1937)

Rockefeller's father sold "miracle cures," and John started young in the business world. Attracted by the Pennsylvania "oil rush," he founded the Standard Oil Company, which by the end of the 19th century dominated the U.S. oil industry. In 1896, after becoming the richest man in the world, he left the company to his son and donated part of his fortune to various foundations—particularly for the creation of universities.

Henri Deterding
(1866-1939)

Born in Holland, Deterding went to work in Asia for the Dutch Petroleum Company, which he headed from 1899. Determined to compete with Standard Oil, he joined forces with the British company Shell Oil, forming what was then the world's largest oil-producing business. Nicknamed the "Napoleon of Oil," he managed wells all over the world. As a Nazi supporter, however, he went to live in Germany in 1936 and had to leave the company.

Calouste Gulbenkian

(1869-1955)

An Armenian financier, Gulbenkian was responsible for negotiating concessions with the Ottoman rulers on behalf of the European oil companies. Nicknamed "Mr. 5%" after gaining a 5% share in the Turkish Petroleum Company, he accumulated a vast fortune and a huge art collection. He spent his last years in Portugal and left his art collection to the government when he died.

Abdelaziz ben Abderrahmane Al Saoud

(ca. 1880-1953)

After 30 years of fighting, Al Saoud founded modern Saudi Arabia in 1932 and became its first King. The discovery of oil in 1938 made Saudi Arabia one of the world's major producers, and Al Saoud made an alliance with the Americans, who would manage the country's oil supplies and provide it with military protection—an agreement that continued after his death.

The oil-rich United Arab Emirates

In the 1960s, huge reserves of oil and gas were discovered in a strip of land situated between the Persian Gulf and Saudi Arabia.

IRAQ
IRAN
AFGHANISTAN
KUWAIT
PAKISTAN
SAUDI ARABIA
DUBAI
ABU DHABI
UNITED ARAB EMIRATES

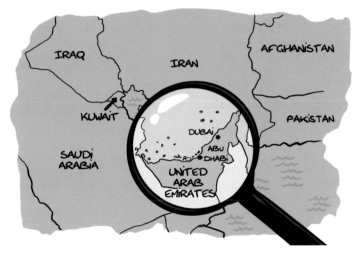

The **seven emirs** (Arab tribal leaders) who then ruled over the area decided to join forces in order to exploit these resources, and they founded the **United Arab Emirates** in 1971.

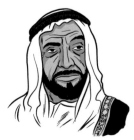

The country's founding President is Zayed ben Sultan Al Nahyane, emir of Abu Dhabi (the country's capital), where the largest oil reserves can be found. Born in a village in the desert, Al Nahyane led the country until his death in 2004 and was responsible for the development of its oil industry, which made him one of the richest men in the world.

Part of the wealth generated by the oil industry is distributed among the people of the UAE: **the state gives all citizens a house, as well as free education and health care**. But most (almost 85%) of the UAE's inhabitants are not citizens; they're foreigners, and they live and work in difficult conditions. Oil revenues have enabled the government to build ultra-modern cities, and, at over

The Burj Khalifa tower in Dubai has 163 stories.

2,700 feet, the **Burj Khalifa** tower in Dubai has been the world's tallest building since its construction in 2008.

But oil revenues will not last forever, and the Emirates are now looking to other sources of income, such as tourism. The **Louvre Abu Dhabi**, a museum of art and civilization, was opened by agreement with the French government in 2017.

The Louvre Abu Dhabi.

Oil and pollution

Deep drilling is needed to extract oil from the ground, and the gasses that escape from oil wells must be burned off. Both activities cause considerable pollution. The rivers near the wells at Khanty-Mansiysk in Siberia are so polluted that local people can no longer eat the fish, and the snow is no longer white, but gray!

Pump jacks in Siberia.

Shipping accidents sometimes cause toxic "**oil slicks**," which can pollute coastlines and kill birds, coating their feathers with sticky oil. In 1999, the oil tanker "Erika" ran aground off the coast of Brittany, France, polluting 250 miles of shoreline; and in 2010, 11 people died when the "Deepwater Horizon" drilling platform in the Gulf of Mexico exploded, releasing 3 million barrels of oil into the sea and onto 1,250 miles of coastline.

Oil slicks can kill tens of thousands of seabirds by gluing their feathers together.

Oil is burned in engines and factories, which adds to the amount of carbon dioxide (CO_2) in the air. This leads to a "**greenhouse effect**," where the Earth's heat is "trapped" in the atmosphere—an effect that can have a negative impact on the planet's climate: for example, causing more frequent storms and turning more areas of land into desert.

Plastic, which is made from petroleum, is not bio-degradable, and growing "**plastic continents**," made up of millions of plastic objects that have been thrown away, can be seen floating on the Earth's oceans and drifting with the currents.

NORTH ATLANTIC
NORTH PACIFIC
SOUTH PACIFIC
SOUTH ATLANTIC
INDIAN OCEAN

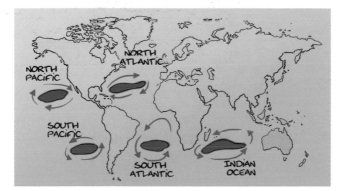

Timeline

The first oil wells
are dug in Baku
(Azerbaijan).

▼

1847

Edwin Drake designs
the first oil well in the
United States, starting
the "oil rush."

▼

1859

1935

1918-1922

▲

Nylon, a synthetic
fiber made from oil,
is invented.

▲

Britain and France
share the territory (and oil
reserves) of the former
Ottoman Empire.

1939-1941

1944

▲

The control of oil
supplies helps the Allies
defeat the Nazis.

▲

Aramco is founded, and
America takes control of
Saudi Arabia's oil supplies.

John Davison Rockefeller founds the Standard Oil Company.

▼

1870

The German Gottlieb Daimler invents the internal combustion engine.

▼

1885

1914-1918

▲

Oil becomes an international weapon during the First World War.

1903

▲

The first oil fields are discovered in Persia.

1945-1973

▲

The European and American economies enjoy an unprecedented boom thanks to oil.

1991

▲

Gulf War.

WATCH OUT FOR PAPERCUTZ

Welcome to the time-travelling third volume of MAGICAL HISTORY TOUR #3 "Hidden Oil," by Fabrice Erre and Sylvain Savoia, from Papercutz, those consumers of too many plastic toys dedicated to publishing great graphic novels for all ages. I'm Jim Salicrup, the Editor-in-Chief and Carbon Lifeform here to further enlighten you regarding the secrets of hidden oil...

"But, Jim," I can hear you saying, "Annie and Nico (mostly Annie) just told us the utterly fascinating history of oil, what could you possibly hope to add?" Well, that's true, and actually I really want to elaborate on what they told you way back on page 4—that oil is "made up of plants and animals that ended up on the ocean floor. Over time, they got covered with 'sediment' (that's tiny particles of rock, like sand), which acted like a pressure cooker... and formed 'pockets' of oil." So, the unasked question is: exactly what kinds of animals and plants? The answer is hinted at on page 5, panel 2, where we see Nico and Annie walking above ground where not far below them are the bones of a dinosaur, and Annie says, "The process of turning plants into oil takes millions of years. It started long before human beings existed." The answer therefore is prehistoric plant life and dinosaurs.

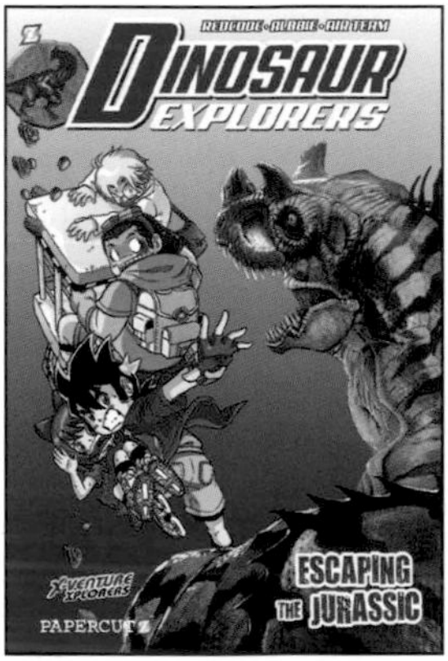
DINOSAUR
EXPLORERS
ESCAPING THE JURASSIC
PAPERCUTZ

©2021 KADOKAWA GEMPAK STARZ

Now if you're the insatiably curious type, you may also want to know from where those plants and dinosaurs came. That's a really tough question. There have been many theories over the years, and the latest theory is presented in the Papercutz graphic novel series DINOSAUR EXPLORERS. Like MAGICAL HISTORY TOUR, each DINOSAURS EXPLORERS graphic novel takes you back in time. In fact, the first two volumes take us back to the time before dinosaurs, where we meet the animals and plant life that existed on Earth then. And every volume of DINOSAUR EXPLORERS reveals the current scientific theory of how the Earth itself was created.

Before the creation of Earth, however, we got nothing. Literally. But if you join us again for the next MAGICAL HISTORY TOUR, Annie and Nico will be more than happy to tell you all about "The Crusades." And we know that a seeker of knowledge such as yourself will not want to miss that!

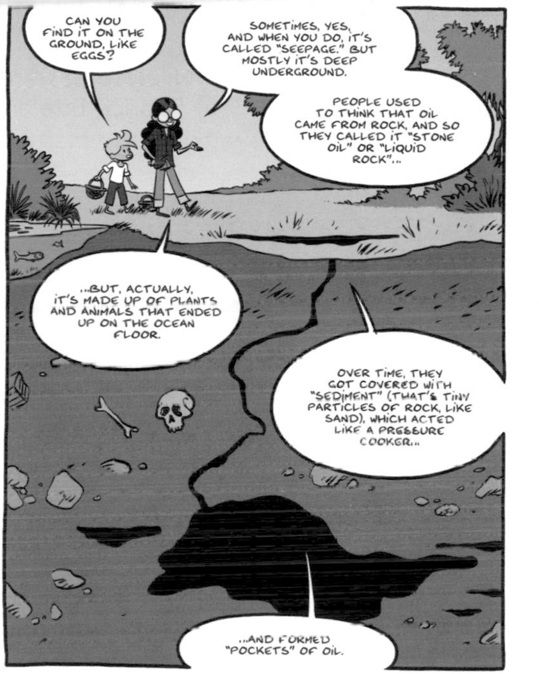

CAN YOU FIND IT ON THE GROUND, LIKE EGGS?
SOMETIMES, YES, AND WHEN YOU DO, IT'S CALLED "SEEPAGE." BUT MOSTLY IT'S DEEP UNDERGROUND.
PEOPLE USED TO THINK THAT OIL CAME FROM ROCK, AND SO THEY CALLED IT "STONE OIL" OR "LIQUID ROCK"...
...BUT, ACTUALLY, IT'S MADE UP OF PLANTS AND ANIMALS THAT ENDED UP ON THE OCEAN FLOOR.
OVER TIME, THEY GOT COVERED WITH "SEDIMENT" (THAT'S TINY PARTICLES OF ROCK, LIKE SAND), WHICH ACTED LIKE A PRESSURE COOKER...
...AND FORMED "POCKETS" OF OIL.

Thanks, Jim

STAY IN TOUCH!

EMAIL:	salicrup@papercutz.com
WEB:	www.papercutz.com
TWITTER:	@papercutzgn
INSTAGRAM:	@papercutzgn
FACEBOOK:	PAPERCUTZGRAPHICNOVELS
FANMAIL:	Papercutz, 160 Broadway, Suite 700, East Wing, New York, NY 10038

Go to papercutz.com and sign up for the free Papercutz e-newsletter!

Fabrice Erre has a Ph.D. in History and teaches Geography and History at the Lycee Jean Jaures near Montpellier, France. He has written a thesis on the satirical press, writes the blog *Une annee au lycee (A Year in High School)* on the website of *Le Monde*, one of France's top national newspapers, and has published several comics.

Sylvain Savoia draws the *Marzi* series, which tells the history of Poland as seen through the eyes of a child. He has also drawn *Les esclaves oublies de Tromelin (The Forgotten Slaves of Tromelin)*, which won the *Academie de Marine de Paris* prize.

MORE GREAT GRAPHIC NOVEL SERIES AVAILABLE FROM PAPERCUTZ™

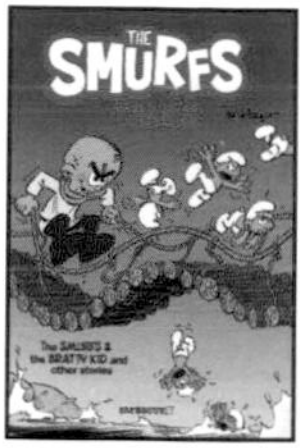
THE SMURFS
THE SMURFS TALES #1

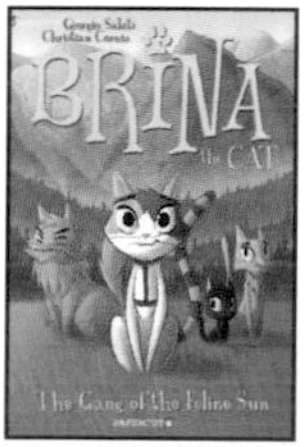
BRINA THE CAT
The Gang of the Feline Sun
BRINA THE CAT #1

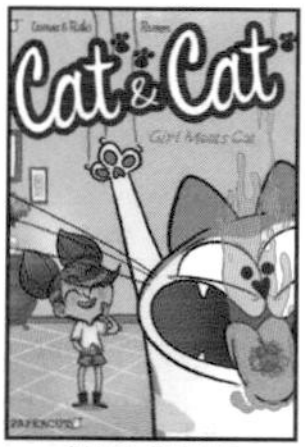
Cat & Cat
Girl Meets Cat
CAT & CAT #1

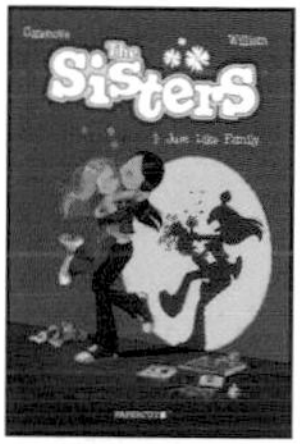
The Sisters
THE SISTERS #1

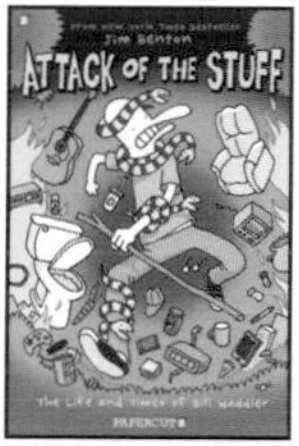
Jim Benton
ATTACK OF THE STUFF
ATTACK OF THE STUFF

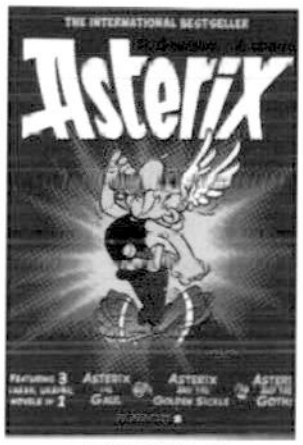
Asterix
ASTERIX #1

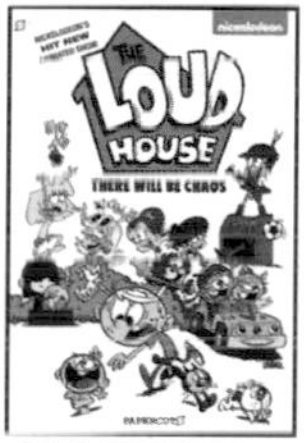
The Loud House
THERE WILL BE CHAOS
THE LOUD HOUSE #1

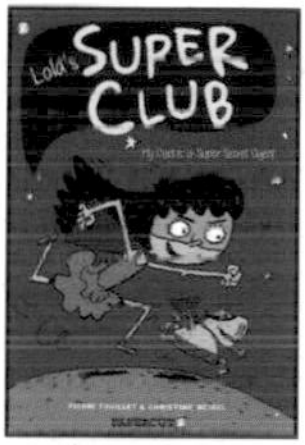
Lola's SUPER CLUB
LOLA'S SUPER CLUB #1

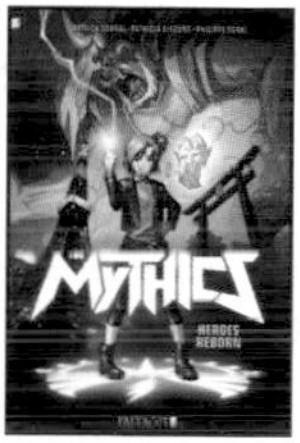
MYTHICS
HEROES REBORN
THE MYTHICS #1

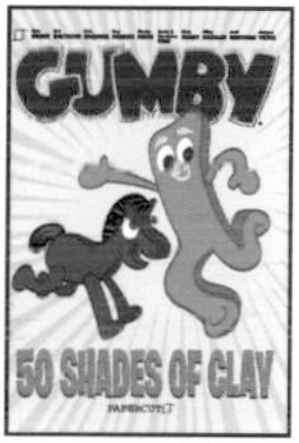
GUMBY
50 SHADES OF CLAY
GUMBY #1

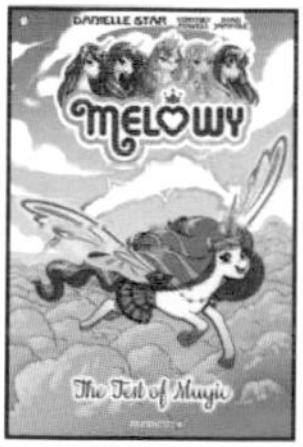
Melowy
The Test of Magic
MELOWY #1

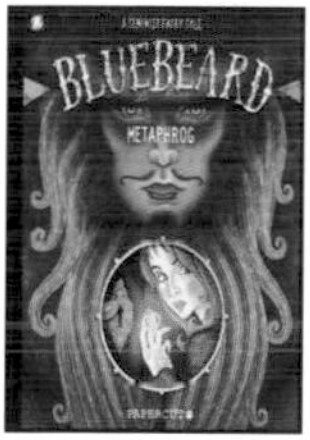
BLUEBEARD
METAPHROG
BLUEBEARD

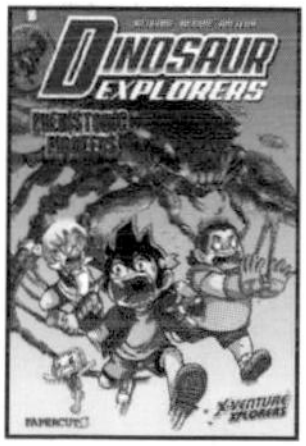
Dinosaur Explorers
DINOSAUR EXPLORERS #1

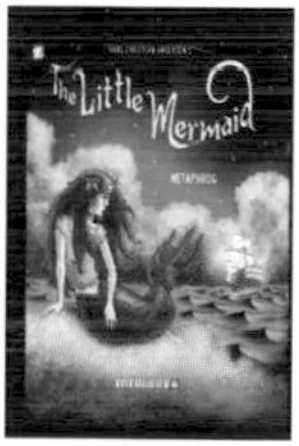
The Little Mermaid
METAPHROG
THE LITTLE MERMAID

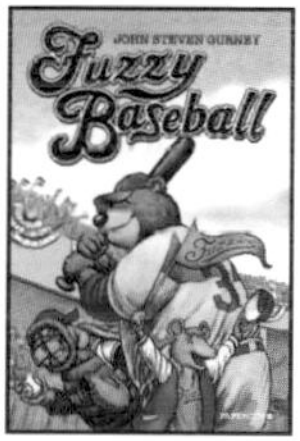
JOHN STEVEN GURNEY
Fuzzy Baseball
FUZZY BASEBALL #1

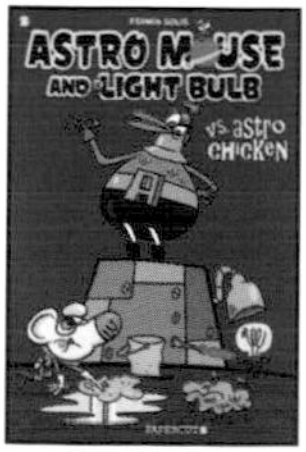
ASTRO MOUSE AND LIGHT BULB
VS. ASTRO CHICKEN
ASTRO MOUSE AND LIGHT BULB #1

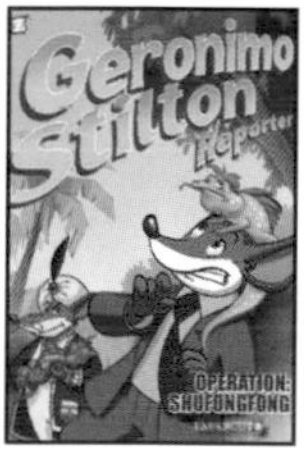
Geronimo Stilton
Reporter
OPERATION: SHUFONGFONG
GERONIMO STILTON REPORTER #1

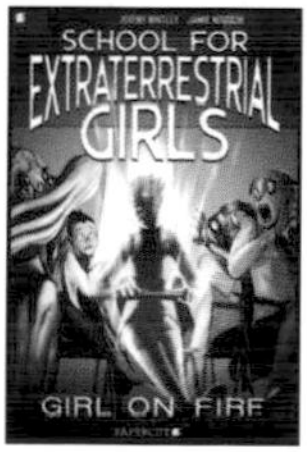
SCHOOL FOR EXTRATERRESTRIAL GIRLS
GIRL ON FIRE
SCHOOL FOR EXTRA-TERRESTRIAL GIRLS #1

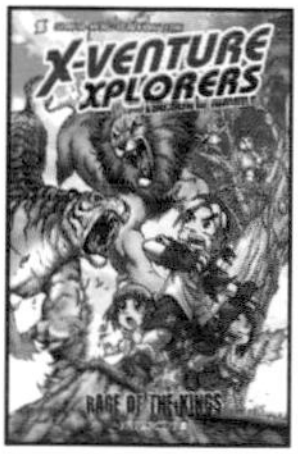
X-VENTURE XPLORERS
RAGE OF THE KINGS
X-VENTURE XPLORERS #1

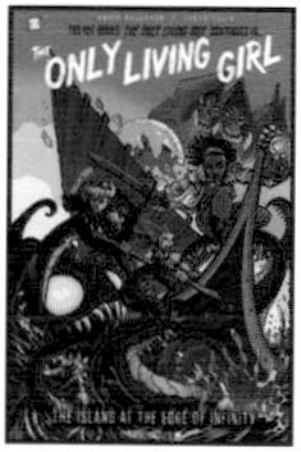
THE ONLY LIVING GIRL
THE ONLY LIVING GIRL #1

papercutz.com

Also available where ebooks are sold.